The Best of Casual French Cooking

BISTRO

SUNSET BOOKS
President and Publisher: Susan J. Maruyama
Director, Finance and Business Affairs: Gary Loebner
Director, Manufacturing and Sales Service: Lorinda Reichert
Director, Sales and Marketing: Richard A. Smeby
Editorial Director: Kenneth Winchester
Executive Editor: Robert A. Doyle

SUNSET PUBLISHING CORPORATION
Chairman: Jim Nelson
President/Chief Executive Officer: Robin Wolaner
Chief Financial Officer: James E. Mitchell
Publisher: Stephen J. Seabolt
Circulation Director: Robert I. Gursha
Editor, *Sunset Magazine:* William R. Marken

Produced by
WELDON OWEN INC.
President: John Owen
Publisher/Vice President: Wendely Harvey
Managing Editor and Introductory Text: Lisa Chaney Atwood
Consulting Editor: Norman Kolpas
Copy Editor: Sharon Silva
Design: Patty Hill
Production Director: Stephanie Sherman
Production Editor: Janique Gascoigne
Co-Editions Director: Derek Barton
Co-Editions Production Manager (US): Tarji Mickelson
Food Photography: Peter Johnson
Assistant Food Photographer: Dal Harper
Food Stylist: Janice Baker
Assistant Food Stylists: Amanda Biffin, Liz Nolan, Alison Turner
Cover Photography: Joyce Oudkerk Pool
Cover Food Stylist: Susan Massey
Cover Prop Stylist: Carol Hacker
Half-Title Illustration: Martha Anne Booth
Chapter Opener Illustrations: Michelle Stong
Glossary Illustrations: Alice Harth

Production by Kyodo Printing Co.
(S'pore) Pte Ltd
Printed in Singapore

ISBN 0-376-02036-9
Library of Congress Catalog Card Number: 95-067089

A Note on Weights and Measures:
All recipes include customary U.S. and metric measurements.
Metric conversions are based on a standard developed for these
books and have been rounded off. Actual weights may vary.

The Best of Casual French Cooking

BISTRO

by Gerald Hirigoyen

Contents

Poultry and Meat 69

Desserts 97

Introduction

*O*pen the door to a good French bistro and you are at once embraced by an atmosphere of clamorous activity—aproned waiters shouting orders to the kitchen, the clink of steel to white china, the steady hum of conversation. Whisked through the crowd and seated at a favorite table, customers are invited to relax and enjoy good food—a welcome end to a busy day.

Bistros are primarily neighborhood restaurants, offering simple fare at an honest price. They draw a mostly local clientele, who find comfort in the lively, yet intimate environment and familiar menu. Waiters know many of their customers by name, and feel compelled to suggest the best seasonal specialties or to point out changes in the menu that might affect their regular orders.

Through the swinging doors of a bistro kitchen come deftly prepared dishes that often include ingredients evocative of the region in which they are served. Contemporary menus routinely pair the hearty braises and stews favored in earlier years with the lighter and fresher preparations so popular today.

The bistro's continuing appeal lies in this unerring balance of contemporary and classic culinary styles. Add to that its unassuming atmosphere and homespun comforts, and it is easy to understand what keeps bistros thriving year after year.

Bistro History

The origin of the word *bistro* is obscure. One theory attributes it to the Russian word *bistro* ("quick"), which the Cossacks shouted as they crowded into the cafés and restaurants of Paris during their occupation of the city in 1815. Other scholars link the word to *bistrouille,* which means "to blend inferior wines." Still others compare it to *bistreau,* which, in the dialect of western France, denotes a cowherd, a person thought of as particularly jolly, much like the barkeeps in the early bistros of provincial France.

The first bistros evolved as places for working people to eat quickly and efficiently in and around Les Halles, the once-famous market district of Paris. The kitchens of these early establishments were primarily the domain of welcoming older women familiarly referred to as *mères* (mothers) and of their cooking, known as *cuisine de mères.*

As the appreciation for the simple fare and informal atmosphere of bistros grew, so did their numbers. By the mid-1800s, neighborhood bistros were

popping up in nearly every district of the capital. Along with the city's laborers, these early eateries also drew many intellectuals and artists, who migrated from the cafés at mealtimes to eat the uncomplicated, inexpensive dishes characteristic of bistro dining. So distinctive was the nature of the bistro that a number of writers, such as Emile Zola in the nineteenth century and Ernest Hemingway and F. Scott Fitzgerald in the twentieth, immortalized this uniquely French institution by describing it as a setting for dozens of novels and short stories.

The Bistro Experience

Today, the bistro continues to hold some of its earlier bohemian appeal. Most still retain the intimate and unassuming ambiance of the first bistros in Paris, offering neither the stark informality of a café nor the luxurious appointments of a fine restaurant. The best are expert in providing their regular customers with a home away from home. Since bistros are usually neighborhood haunts, the most successful offer an atmosphere that meshes with that of their principal clientele. In Paris, those in the Latin Quarter are dominated by the cacophonous ambiance and spare surroundings sought after by the many students who frequent that neighborhood. Along the fashionable Rue St. Honoré, shoppers flock to any of a string of trendy, brightly colored bistros at lunchtime.

The most traditional bistros are found in the residential neighborhoods, where the understated eateries cater to the repeat business of local residents. Between a long banquette and rows of simple wooden chairs are tables covered in starched linen and topped with a seamless layer of white butcher paper. Lace curtains filter light from windows facing the street. Warm wood paneling imparts a sense of confidentiality and reassurance. On large chalkboards behind the bar, *les plats du jour* are written in a bold European hand.

Bistro Fare

With few exceptions, these neighborhood establishments continue to offer a number of the dishes that made them famous. Regulars can rest assured that specialties such as steak tartare, onion tart and the hearty cassoulet of Languedoc still find space on the menus of modern bistros.

In addition to their own renditions of classic French favorites, the best bistro chefs continually incorporate a range of lesser known ingredients, as well as lessons and techniques from many different cultures. Indeed, French chefs have historically been among the first to experiment with new spices and ingredients. Flavorful additions such as saffron, once limited in Europe to the kitchens of Spain and Italy, and the curry powder of India have become commonplace in French cuisine. Also seen with increasing frequency are tropical fruits like mango and papaya and different varieties of fish and shellfish.

In France, the largest meal is traditionally served midday and many French citizens take a full two-hour lunch break in order to savor it fully. A complete bistro meal, although less structured than those of haute cuisine, commonly includes three courses; special occasions and Sunday midday repasts see the number rise to four or five. The basic menu commences with a small appetizer, usually cold, followed by a main dish, either fish or meat, and lastly cheeses and fruit or a simple dessert.

A loaf of the local bread is a necessary accompaniment to each savory course. Slices from the loaf are often eaten plain, used in part for sopping up any juices or flavorful sauces that remain on the plate.

Bringing the Bistro Home

It is easy to re-create a bistro environment in your own home. Put together a menu based upon any of the classic and contemporary French recipes on the pages that follow and shop for the best seasonal ingredients in your local market. You might also arrange a variety of local cheeses on a tray lined with fresh grape leaves. Then set your table with fresh, white linens,

plain porcelain dishware and well-worn silver, and arrange a few flowers in a simple vase for an understated centerpiece. Offer a French vintage that subtly complements the dishes you are serving and you will have set the stage for a true Gallic feast.

Beverages

Not surprisingly, the French take their choice of drink seriously and nothing is considered a better accompaniment to any type of meal than the appropriate wine. For everyday dining, a glass of the local vintage poured from a large barrel behind the bar will suffice. But, for the well-crafted meals reserved for special occasions and long Sunday afternoons, the selection of a beverage to complement the characteristics of each course takes on considerable importance. Such celebrations usually include a few different vintages, along with an aperitif, still or carbonated water and sometimes a digestif.

Aperitifs

Cocktails before dining are seldom the choice of bistro habitués. Of the distilled liquors, scotch, served in tumblers straight up or on the rocks, is the most popular choice. Women often prefer light aperitifs poured into small stemmed glasses. Semi-dry, wine-based *Lillet* is a typical selection, as are sherry and port. A glass of wine or a *kir* (opposite) is also a nice way to begin a meal.

Many bistros also offer a variety of locally brewed aperitifs. *Pastis,* for example, a strong anise-flavored drink, is especially popular in the south. Indeed, throughout France residents enjoy their own local liqueurs or regional combinations of fortified wine, herbs and spices. Many French claim that such exceptionally strong spirits, drunk plain or with water, are the key to nurturing a healthy appetite.

Wine

In bistro culture, discovering the perfect match of wine to food is more passion than pastime. Yet even the most ardent oenologist finds the task a formidable challenge. There are hundreds of different wines bottled in France alone, each with characteristics that vary not only according to region and classification, but also to soil, climate, grape varietals, age and vinification. When in doubt, ask your waiter to guide you.

One good rule to follow when pairing wine with food is to match the intensity of flavors. For example, if a dish is spicy, select a full-bodied vintage to equal its spirited savor, such as a fruity Gewürztraminer from Alsace or a robust red Bordeaux. If a recipe itself calls for wine, select the same type of wine for the table.

White wines are traditionally drunk to accompany the first course and fish, shellfish, poultry and light meat dishes. An Alsatian Riesling or a Chablis or other white Bordeaux would be appropriate for the lightest

of these offerings, a zestier dry Sancerre or Muscadet would mate well with more flavorful shellfish, and a Gewürztraminer would be a fine match for the complex character of a pâté or perfectly ripe Roquefort.

Robust red wines, such as those from Bordeaux and the Côte du Rhône are generally best with dark meats and rich sauces. Burgundies can be light or heavy: A mild, fruity Beaujolais suits a light veal, fish or poultry preparation, while a slightly heavier red from the Côte des Nuits complements lamb, duck and more flavorful poultry and veal dishes.

Coffee and Digestifs

In France, coffee rarely accompanies food—not even dessert. Instead, it is served after the meal has ended, commonly black and very strong, in small, white espresso cups. Although once reserved only for breakfast, coffee with steamed milk, as in *café au lait*, is now seen on some bistro menus.

Some claim that nothing settles the stomach like a snifter of brandy or a glass of eau-de-vie. French brandies distilled from grapes, such as Cognac and Armagnac, are prized for their subtle depth of flavor, rich amber color and complex aroma. Calvados, an apple brandy from Normandy, is a popular alternative to grape distillates and is often served in small quantities at the meal's end.

Eau-de-vie, literally "water of life," applies to a range of spirits distilled from fruits and herbs. Among the most popular varieties are those made from raspberry *(framboise)*, prune *(prunelle)* and pear *(poire)*.

Beer

In France, beer is not usually consumed with food, unless the dish in question is particularly spicy or from the beer-producing region of Alsace. Instead, beer is more popularly enjoyed on its own or with a snack in the mid-afternoon or at the end of a workday.

KIR

This simple concoction is named after Canon Kir, a mayor of Dijon, who died in 1968. The traditional kir combines crème de cassis (a black currant liqueur) and white wine. For a special occasion, a kir royale, a mixture of crème de cassis and chilled Champagne, may be served. And, in some cafés, one can find the communard, a blend of cassis and red wine.

1 tablespoon crème de cassis
½ cup (4 fl oz/125 ml) dry white wine, chilled
Lemon zest strip

Pour the crème de cassis into a tall tulip glass. Add the white wine and stir gently to mix. Garnish with a twist of lemon zest and serve.

Serves 1

INTRODUCTION

Basic Recipes

Bistro chefs keep a few staples on hand to draw upon in their cooking. Flavorful meat stocks are often left simmering on the stove top to use as needed. And, stored in the refrigerator, one may expect to find a good vinaigrette and fresh tomato sauce, as well as sweet fillings for desserts and tart shells ready for baking.

CHICKEN STOCK
FOND DE VOLAILLE

Homemade chicken stock provides a flavorful base for a range of soups, stews, sauces and braises. Enterprising home cooks can have fresh stock on hand simply by making the stock ahead and freezing it in small freezer bags to use as needed.

2   white onions
4   whole cloves
    Bouquet garni *(see glossary, page 124)*
6   lb (3 kg) chicken carcasses
2   large carrots, peeled and coarsely chopped
3   celery stalks, coarsely chopped
10 cloves garlic
1   tablespoon whole black peppercorns

✣ Coarsely chop 1 of the onions. Stud the other whole onion with the 4 cloves.

✣ In a stockpot, combine all the ingredients and add water just to cover (about 3¾ qt/3.75 l). Bring to a boil and, using a large spoon or wire skimmer, skim off any foam that forms on the surface. Reduce the heat to low and simmer, uncovered, for 1–1½ hours, reducing the liquid only slightly. Continue to skim off any foam that floats to the top during simmering.

✣ Strain the stock through a fine-mesh sieve lined with cheesecloth (muslin) into a clean container. Discard the contents of the sieve. Use immediately, or let cool, cover and refrigerate for up to 1 week or freeze for up to 1 month. Lift off any solidified fat from the surface of the chilled stock before using.

Makes about 2½ qt (2.5 l)

VEAL STOCK
FOND DE VEAU

Stocks have a superior flavor when they are prepared in large quantities rather than in small amounts. Since you will probably not use all of this stock at once, however, you can freeze leftover stock in freezer bags or other containers for up to 1 month. For an even more intense flavor, add about 2 pounds (1 kg) oxtails with the veal bones.

8   lb (4 kg) large veal bones, such as leg bones
2   white onions
4   whole cloves
2   large carrots, peeled and coarsely chopped
3   celery stalks, coarsely chopped
10 cloves garlic
⅔   cup (5 fl oz/150 ml) tomato paste
    Bouquet garni *(see glossary, page 124)*
1   tablespoon whole black peppercorns
1   cup (8 fl oz/250 ml) water

🌿 Preheat an oven to 500°F (260°C). Place the veal bones in a roasting pan and roast for 20 minutes.

🌿 Meanwhile, coarsely chop 1 of the onions. Stud the other whole onion with the cloves.

🌿 Remove the pan from the oven and distribute the carrots, chopped and whole onion, celery, garlic and tomato paste evenly over the veal bones. Return to the oven and roast until the vegetables are lightly browned, about 15 minutes.

🌿 Using a slotted spoon, transfer all the contents of the roasting pan to a stockpot. Add the bouquet garni and peppercorns. Discard the fat from the roasting pan and place the pan over medium heat. When the pan is hot, add the water and deglaze the pan by stirring to dislodge any browned bits from the pan bottom. Pour the liquid into the stockpot.

🌿 Add water to the stockpot just to cover the ingredients (about 6 qt/6 l). Bring to a boil and, using a large spoon or a wire skimmer, skim off any foam that forms on top. Reduce the heat to low, cover and simmer for about 3 hours. Continue to skim off any foam that floats to the top during simmering.

🌿 Strain the stock through a fine-mesh sieve lined with cheesecloth (muslin) into a clean container. Discard the contents of the sieve.

🌿 Use immediately, or let cool, cover and refrigerate for up to 1 week or freeze for up to 1 month. Lift off any solidified fat from the surface of the chilled stock before using.

Makes about 3½ qt (3.5 l)

VIÑAIGRETTE
VINAIGRETTE

Many bistros provide oil and vinegar in separate cruets on the table for guests to mix together to taste. This recipe eliminates the guesswork, providing a good, basic vinaigrette that should suit any variety of uses.

2 tablespoons sherry vinegar
2 tablespoons balsamic vinegar
1 teaspoon salt
¼ teaspoon ground white pepper
⅔ cup (5 fl oz/150 ml) olive oil

🌿 In a small bowl, using a wire whisk, whisk together the sherry and balsamic vinegars, salt and white pepper.

🌿 Whisking continuously, add the olive oil in a slow, steady stream, whisking until well blended and emulsified, about 1 minute.

Makes about 1 cup (8 fl oz/250 ml)

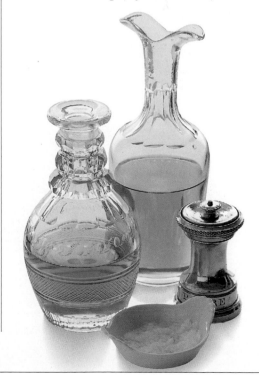

TOMATO AND RED PEPPER COULIS
COULIS DE TOMATES AUX POIVRONS ROUGE

The term coulis *refers to a liquid purée of cooked seasoned vegetables. Although delicious as a sauce on its own, a coulis can also be used to enhance other sauces and provide added flavor to an assortment of dishes. With the addition of a little olive oil and vinegar, it makes an excellent vinaigrette as well. If the coulis seems too thick, simply add water until you achieve the desired consistency.*

3   tablespoons olive oil
1   white onion, coarsely chopped
2   small red bell peppers (capsicums), seeded, deribbed and coarsely chopped
5   cloves garlic
3   tomatoes, coarsely chopped
    Bouquet garni *(see glossary, page 124)*
⅛   teaspoon cayenne pepper
1   teaspoon salt, plus salt to taste
¼   teaspoon ground white pepper, plus ground white pepper to taste
⅓   cup (3 fl oz/80 ml) water

⚜ In a large saucepan over high heat, warm the olive oil. Add the onion, bell peppers and garlic and sauté until golden brown, about 10 minutes.

⚜ Add the tomatoes, bouquet garni, cayenne, the 1 teaspoon salt, the ¼ teaspoon white pepper and the water and bring to a boil. Reduce the heat to medium, cover, and simmer gently until thickened, about 45 minutes.

⚜ Working in batches, transfer the mixture to a blender or to a food processor fitted with the metal blade and purée until smooth, about 2 minutes. Taste and adjust the seasoning. Use immediately, or store in an airtight container in the refrigerator for up to 1 week or freeze for up to 1 month.

Makes 2½–3 cups (20–24 fl oz/ 625–750 ml)

SWEET PASTRY DOUGH
PÂTE SUCRÉE

Dense, buttery and rich, this sweet dough makes an ideal tart shell. If you like, you can prepare it ahead to use later; wrapped airtight in plastic wrap, it will keep in the refrigerator for up to 2 weeks.

½   cup (4 oz/125 g) plus 1 tablespoon unsalted butter, at room temperature, cut into pieces
½   cup (2 oz/60 g) confectioners' (icing) sugar, sifted
1   egg
2   cups (10 oz/315 g) all-purpose (plain) flour
⅛   teaspoon baking powder

⚜ In a bowl, combine the butter and sugar. Using an electric mixer set on low speed, beat until smooth, about 3 minutes.

⚜ Add the egg and beat until creamy. Using a rubber spatula, fold in the flour and baking powder just until incorporated. Then beat with the electric mixer set on low speed until the dough is evenly mixed and clings together, 2–3 minutes.

⚜ Shape the dough into a ball, wrap tightly in plastic wrap and refrigerate for at least 2 hours or as long as 2 weeks. Bring to room temperature before using, then use as directed in individual recipes.

Makes enough dough for one 10-inch (25-cm) tart shell

PASTRY CREAM

CRÈME PÂTISSIÈRE

French pastry chefs use this cream as a filling for cakes and pastries, as a garnish and as an addition to hot and cold desserts. Because this recipe calls only for egg yolks, and no whites, it has an especially rich texture. You can make this pastry cream up to 1 day in advance and store it, covered, in the refrigerator.

4   egg yolks
½   cup (4 oz/125 g) sugar
⅓   cup (2 oz/60 g) plus 1 tablespoon all-purpose (plain) flour
2   cups (16 fl oz/500 ml) milk
½   vanilla bean (pod), split in half lengthwise

🌿 In a large bowl, combine the egg yolks and sugar and whisk until thoroughly combined. Add the flour and stir until smooth; set aside.

🌿 In a large saucepan over high heat, combine the milk and the vanilla bean and bring to a boil. As soon as the milk begins to boil, remove it from the heat. Remove the vanilla bean and, using the tip of a small, sharp knife, scrape the seeds directly into the milk. Discard the bean.

🌿 Whisk half of the hot milk into the egg mixture. Return the saucepan to high heat and, as soon as the mixture comes to a boil, pour the contents of the bowl into the saucepan, whisking constantly.

🌿 Using a wooden spoon, stir over high heat until the mixture is smooth. Return to a boil and boil, stirring, for 2 minutes longer.

🌿 Remove the pan from the heat and press a piece of plastic wrap directly onto the surface of the hot cream to prevent a skin from forming. Let cool completely before using.

Makes 2¼ cups (18 fl oz/560 ml)

First Courses

*M*eals in France traditionally open with a simple first course, designed to excite the senses and to prepare the diner for the heartier, and frequently more elaborate, main course that follows. Often served cold and always tasty and light, it aims, after all, not to fill, but merely to tantalize.

Fresh seasonal vegetables, briefly cooked then served cold with a vinaigrette or other light sauce, are a popular choice. Most bistros also offer a range of fresh shellfish, with mollusks usually served on the half shell nested in ice and crustaceans cracked but still in their armor. If a pâté or terrine is ordered, it commonly arrives at the table still in its earthenware vessel, with a loaf of fresh bread alongside for diners to help themselves. In the winter months, creamy soups and lightly browned gratins are favored.

More complex preparations are usually reserved for Sunday dining and special occasions. At such meals, the entrées display a bit more refinement than most daily offerings. One might begin with a crisp layered potato galette, for example, or a savory seafood salad. Dishes are often selected not only for their own individual characteristics, but also with a mind to the roles they play in the meal as a whole.

SOUPE À L'OIGNON GRATINÉE

Onion Soup Gratinée

*In the past, this hearty onion soup with melted cheese on top was served from the late-night hours
into the early morning in the Les Halles market district of Paris. Now, it is served at all times of the day in
France. Commonly referred to as one of the great* soupes de santé, *restorative "soups for the sick," this
flavorful broth is said to work equally well on curing the flu as it does on relieving hangovers.*

3 large white onions
½ cup (4 oz/125 g) unsalted butter
3 tablespoons all-purpose (plain) flour
8 cups (64 fl oz/2 l) beef stock, preferably homemade
Salt and freshly ground pepper
½ day-old baguette
2 cups (8 oz/250 g) shredded Swiss cheese

☙ Cut the onions in half through the stem end, then cut crosswise into thin slices.

☙ In a large saucepan over medium heat, melt the butter. Add the onions and flour and sauté, stirring frequently, until golden brown, about 5 minutes.

☙ Pour in the stock, add salt and pepper to taste and bring to a boil. Reduce the heat to medium and simmer, stirring often, until the onions are soft and translucent and the flavors have blended, about 15 minutes.

☙ Meanwhile, preheat a broiler (griller). Cut the baguette on the diagonal into 6–8 large slices about ½ inch (12 mm) thick.

☙ Ladle the soup into 6–8 ovenproof bowls placed atop a baking sheet. Place a bread slice on top of each serving of soup and scatter the Swiss cheese evenly over the top of the soup and the bread.

☙ Place the baking sheet under the broiler and broil (grill) until the cheese melts and turns golden brown, 2–3 minutes.

☙ Remove from the broiler and serve immediately.

Serves 6–8

Cream of Artichoke Soup

Catherine de' Medicis was the first to popularize artichokes in France when she came to the French court from Italy to marry King Henry II in the late 16th century. In this smooth and mellow soup, only the tender hearts of the artichokes are used. Armagnac adds an extra touch of refinement; if you don't have any on hand, Cognac or any good-quality dry brandy will do.

6 medium-sized artichokes

⅓ cup (3 fl oz/80 ml) olive oil

1 white onion, coarsely chopped

3 celery stalks, coarsely chopped

1 large russet potato, peeled and coarsely chopped

6 cups (48 fl oz/1.5 l) chicken stock *(recipe on page 12)*

⅓ cup (2 oz/60 g) hazelnuts (filberts)

1 tablespoon salt

1 teaspoon ground white pepper

2 cups (16 fl oz/500 ml) heavy (double) cream

⅓ cup (3 fl oz/80 ml) Armagnac

❧ Working with 1 artichoke at a time, cut off the top half. Trim off the stem even with the bottom. Then snap or cut off all the tough outer leaves until you reach the pale green, tender leaves. Carefully spread the tender leaves open and, using a small spoon, remove the prickly choke, leaving the inner leaves intact. Cut each artichoke lengthwise into eighths and set aside.

❧ Preheat an oven to 400°F (200°C).

❧ In a large saucepan over medium-high heat, warm the olive oil. Add the onion and celery and sauté until golden brown, 8–10 minutes. Add the artichokes, potato and chicken stock and bring to a boil. Reduce the heat to medium, cover and simmer until thickened slightly and the flavors have blended, about 45 minutes.

❧ While the soup is cooking, toast and skin the hazelnuts: Spread the nuts in a single layer on a baking sheet and toast in the oven for 5 minutes. Spread the warm nuts on a kitchen towel, cover with another kitchen towel and rub gently against the nuts to remove as much of the skins as possible. Let cool, then chop coarsely and set aside.

❧ Working in batches, transfer the soup to a blender or to a food processor fitted with a metal blade and blend or process on high speed until smooth and creamy, about 1 minute. Strain the puréed soup through a fine-mesh sieve back into the saucepan to remove any fibers. Add the salt, white pepper, cream and Armagnac and bring to a simmer over medium heat, stirring to mix well.

❧ Ladle the soup into warmed bowls and sprinkle with the chopped hazelnuts. Serve immediately.

Serves 6–8

Chestnut and Celery Soup

During the winter months, hot roasted chestnuts are often sold by vendors on the boulevards of Paris. The meaty nut is a popular ingredient in bistros around France, either fresh or as a canned purée. This rich soup—combining chestnut purée with celery, potato and cream— is a popular first course for Christmastime luncheons and New Year's celebrations.

2 cups (1 lb/500 g) prepared unsweetened chestnut purée or 1½ lb (750 g) fresh chestnuts

½ cup (4 oz/125 g) unsalted butter

2 white onions, chopped

3 celery stalks, coarsely chopped

1 large russet potato, peeled and coarsely chopped

6 cups (48 fl oz/1.5 l) chicken stock *(recipe on page 12)*

2 cups (16 fl oz/500 ml) heavy (double) cream

1 tablespoon salt

1 teaspoon ground white pepper

♣ If you are using prepared chestnut purée, set aside. If you are using fresh chestnuts, preheat an oven to 400°F (200°C). Using a sharp knife, cut an X on the flat side of each chestnut. Spread the chestnuts in a shallow pan and roast until the nuts feel tender when pressed and the shells have curled where cut, 25–30 minutes. Remove from the oven and, using a small, sharp knife, remove the shells and the furry skin directly under them. (The nuts peel easiest when still warm.) Set aside.

♣ In a large saucepan over medium-high heat, melt the butter. Add the onions and celery and sauté until golden brown, about 5 minutes.

♣ Add the chestnut purée or roasted chestnuts, potato, chicken stock and cream, stir well and bring to a boil. Add the salt and white pepper, reduce the heat to medium-low and simmer, uncovered, until the soup thickens slightly, about 1 hour.

♣ Working in batches, transfer the soup to a blender and blend on high speed until smooth and creamy, about 1 minute.

♣ Return the soup to the saucepan and bring to a simmer over medium heat. Taste and adjust the seasoning. Ladle into warmed bowls and serve immediately.

Serves 6–8

Salmon Rillettes

Although classic rillettes are commonly prepared with fatty mixtures of pork or duck, this lighter and more contemporary version combines two forms of salmon with lemon juice and chives. Like traditional rillettes, the shredded mixture is served on small buttered toasts as a first course. This dish is excellent accompanied with a cold, crisp glass of Champagne or a dry white wine such as Chenin Blanc.

Salt and freshly ground pepper
13 oz (410 g) fresh salmon fillet, skin removed
½ cup (4 oz/125 g) plus 1½ tablespoons unsalted butter, at room temperature, cut into small pieces
2 eggs
1 teaspoon fresh lemon juice
1 tablespoon chopped fresh chives
7 oz (220 g) sliced smoked salmon, cut into small pieces
Buttered, toasted baguette slices

❦ Rub salt and pepper to taste on both sides of the salmon fillet. Place on a steamer rack over (not touching) gently boiling water. Cover and steam until firm, pale pink and opaque throughout, about 7 minutes, depending upon the thickness. Alternatively, fill a shallow saucepan or sauté pan about half full with water (enough to cover the salmon). Add the salmon and poach until it tests done, about 10 minutes.

❦ Transfer the steamed or poached salmon to a bowl. Shred the salmon thoroughly with a fork and remove any small bones. Cover and refrigerate until cool.

❦ Place the butter in a large mixing bowl and work it with a rubber spatula until it is smooth and creamy. Add the eggs, lemon juice, chives and salt and pepper to taste and mix well. Add the cooled fresh salmon and the smoked salmon and mix together thoroughly.

❦ Spoon the salmon mixture into a terrine or individual ramekins and cover with plastic wrap. Refrigerate for at least 3 hours or as long as overnight. Bring to room temperature before serving.

❦ To serve, spread the salmon mixture on toasted baguette slices.

Serves 6–8

25

Chicken Liver Terrine

Served simply with a baguette or crackers, a liver terrine is a standard prelude to many classic French meals. In many neighborhood bistros, modest terrines like this one are often set right on the table with a loaf of bread, allowing the diners to help themselves before the main course arrives. Soaking the livers in milk overnight removes any bitter flavor and keeps them tasting fresh and rich.

1½ lb (750 g) chicken livers, trimmed of any connective tissue
Milk
1 teaspoon salt
½ teaspoon ground white pepper
1½ cups (12 fl oz/375 ml) heavy (double) cream
1 egg
2 fresh thyme sprigs
2 bay leaves
Toasted baguette slices or crackers (savory biscuits)

❧ The night before you bake the terrine, combine the chicken livers in a shallow bowl with milk to cover. Cover and refrigerate overnight.

❧ The next day, preheat an oven to 375°F (190°C).

❧ Drain the chicken livers and place in a food processor fitted with the metal blade or in a blender. Add the salt, white pepper, cream and egg. Process or blend on high speed until smooth, about 1 minute.

❧ Strain the liver purée through a medium-mesh sieve into a bowl, to remove any fibrous matter. Then pour the strained purée into a 9½-by-3½-by-3½-inch (24-by-9-by-9-cm) terrine. Lay the thyme sprigs and the bay leaves on top as a garnish.

❧ Cover the terrine with its lid or aluminum foil. Place it in a baking pan and pour enough hot water into the pan to reach halfway up the sides of the terrine. Bake until a knife inserted into the center comes out clean, about 45 minutes. Remove the baking pan from the oven and then remove the terrine from the baking pan. Uncover and let cool. Then cover and refrigerate overnight.

❧ Cut into slices and serve chilled or at room temperature. Accompany with toasts or crackers.

Serves 6–8

26

Onion Pie with Roquefort, Prosciutto and Walnuts

A staple of everyday French cooking, onions are a common ingredient in a variety of dishes featured on bistro menus. Embellished with Roquefort, prosciutto and walnuts, this recipe produces a somewhat more upscale version of the ever-popular onion pie. It is traditionally served either as a first course or alongside a crisp green salad for a light supper.

2 tablespoons olive oil

2 white onions, very thinly sliced

¼ cup (2 fl oz/60 ml) water

3 oz (90 g) Roquefort cheese, crumbled into small pieces
   Salt and freshly ground pepper

½ cup (2 oz/60 g) walnuts, coarsely chopped

1 tablespoon unsalted butter, melted

2 puff pastry sheets, each 11 by 15 inches (28 by 37.5 cm), fresh or thawed frozen

1 egg, lightly beaten

4 slices prosciutto, about 1 oz (30 g) each

⚜ Place a baking sheet with sides in a freezer.

⚜ In a sauté pan over medium-high heat, warm the olive oil. Add the onions and sauté until golden brown, about 10 minutes. Add the water and continue to sauté until all the moisture evaporates, about another 5 minutes. Add the Roquefort cheese and continue cooking, stirring occasionally, until melted, about 5 minutes longer. Season only lightly with salt, if needed, and add pepper to taste. Stir in the walnuts, then spread the mixture out onto the chilled sheet pan. Place in the freezer until the onions cool down completely, about 10 minutes.

⚜ Preheat an oven to 450°F (230°C). Brush a baking sheet evenly with the melted butter.

⚜ Place the puff pastry on a cutting board. Using the rim of a small plate about 5 inches (13 cm) in diameter as a guide, cut the pastry into 8 rounds. Discard the pastry scraps.

⚜ Place 4 of the rounds on the prepared baking sheet. Brush their outer rims and tops with the beaten egg. Evenly distribute the cooled onion mixture onto the middle of each of the 4 rounds, leaving 1 inch (2.5 cm) uncovered around the edges. Place 1 prosciutto slice on top of each mound of the onion mixture. Cover each round with a second pastry round, making sure to pinch down firmly around the edges to seal in the filling. Brush the top of each "pie" with more of the beaten egg. Using a small, sharp knife, pierce the top of each pie once with a small slit.

⚜ Bake until golden brown, about 20 minutes. Remove from the oven and serve immediately.

Serves 4

Potato and Goat Cheese Galette

Although many galettes take the form of sweet cakes, the traditional galette of the French countryside is often a savory creation made from finely sliced or puréed potatoes. In this refined first-course preparation, potato rings are filled with fresh goat cheese and then breaded and fried.

Peanut oil or vegetable oil for deep-frying

2 russet potatoes, well scrubbed

6–8 oz (185–250 g) fresh goat cheese

2 pinches of cayenne pepper

½ cup (2 oz/60 g) fine dried bread crumbs

2 oil-packed sun-dried tomatoes, drained and blotted dry

10 large European brine-cured black olives, such as Kalamata

2 tablespoons pure olive oil

1 teaspoon extra-virgin olive oil

4 fresh basil leaves

Freshly ground pepper

🌿 In a deep-fat fryer or a heavy saucepan, pour the peanut or vegetable oil to a depth of 3 inches (7.5 cm). Heat to 300°F (150°C) on a deep-fat frying thermometer, or until a drop of water added to the oil dances and pops on the surface.

🌿 Meanwhile, cut off the ends of the potatoes and discard. Slice the centers of the potatoes crosswise into disks ¾ inch (2 cm) wide. You should have 4 disks in all. Cut a hole out of the center of each potato disk, forming a sturdy "ring." Be sure to leave at least a ½-inch (12-mm) border of potato remaining around the hole.

🌿 Slip the potato rings into the oil and deep-fry until they start to turn golden brown, about 5 minutes. Using a slotted spoon, remove the potato rings from the oil and place on paper towels. Pat the rings dry with the paper towels, removing any excess oil.

🌿 Fill the center of each of the 4 rings with one-fourth of the goat cheese. Smooth the surfaces of the rings by carefully scraping off any protruding cheese with a spatula. Sprinkle both sides of the cheese-filled potato rings with cayenne pepper. Spread the bread crumbs on a

plate and coat both sides of the rings with the crumbs. Place the coated rings in a single layer on another plate, cover with plastic wrap and refrigerate for at least 2 hours or for up to 1 day.

🌿 Just before serving, slice each sun-dried tomato into 8 pieces; cut each olive in half, removing the pit. Place the tomatoes and olives around the outer edges of individual plates, alternating them to form a colorful pattern.

🌿 In a large nonstick sauté pan, warm the pure olive oil. Add the potatoes and cook, turning once, just until they turn golden brown, 20–30 seconds on each side. Transfer the cooked potatoes to the garnished plates.

🌿 Swirl a little of the extra-virgin olive oil evenly over each of the potatoes and the garnish. Place a single basil leaf on the center of each potato and then sprinkle with a few turns of ground pepper. Serve immediately.

Serves 4

Foie Gras Poached in Sweet Wine

In France, the fresh plumped goose or duck liver known as foie gras is often reserved for special occasions. Although foie gras used to be difficult to find outside of France, it can now be purchased in specialty-food stores. Accompany with the same late-harvest sweet wine used for cooking.

1   foie gras, about 1½ lb (750 g)

1⅔ cups (13 fl oz/400 ml) late-harvest sweet wine

2   teaspoons plus 1 tablespoon salt

2   teaspoons ground white pepper

7   cups (56 fl oz/1.75 l) veal stock *(recipe on page 12)* or purchased beef stock

     Ice cubes

1   day-old baguette

⚜ Split apart the 2 lobes of the foie gras and, using a small, sharp knife, remove any thick portions of the veinlike connective tissue running through the lobes.

⚜ Place the lobes of foie gras in a dish and pour ⅔ cup (5 fl oz/150 ml) of the sweet wine over them. Sprinkle each lobe evenly on all sides with the 2 teaspoons salt and 1 teaspoon of the white pepper. Cover with plastic wrap and let marinate in a refrigerator for 2–6 hours (the longer the better), turning the lobes at least 2 or 3 times to ensure that they are evenly flavored.

⚜ Remove the foie gras from the marinade, reserving the marinade, and place in the center of a large piece of cheesecloth (muslin). Wrap the cloth around the lobes and press them gently into a sausage shape. Using kitchen string, tie the cheesecloth-wrapped "roll" of foie gras firmly at both ends. Then tie along the length of the roll every 1½ inches (4 cm), forming a sausage shape about 7–8 inches (18–20 cm) long and 2–2½ inches (5–6 cm) wide.

⚜ In a saucepan, combine the stock, the remaining wine and the reserved marinade. Bring to a boil over medium-high heat and add the remaining salt and white pepper. Then gently drop in the roll of foie gras. Return to a boil and poach gently until slightly tender to the touch, 4–5 minutes.

⚜ Meanwhile, fill a bowl large enough to hold the roll with ice cubes and add a splash of water. When the foie gras is done, using tongs, remove it from the pan and promptly bury it in the bowl of ice to halt the cooking. Let stand for 1 minute, then remove the roll and place it in a deep rectangular terrine or bowl. Place the saucepan holding the stock in the bowl of ice to cool it down completely, about 15 minutes.

⚜ Pour the cooled stock into the terrine or bowl to cover the roll completely. Cover and refrigerate for at least 24 hours or for up to 3 days.

⚜ Just before serving, cut the baguette crosswise into thin slices and toast until golden brown.

⚜ Remove the roll from the stock, snip off the strings, and unwrap the foie gras. To serve, heat a sharp knife by dipping it into hot water. Wipe the blade dry, then slice the foie gras into medallions ¼ inch (6 mm) thick. Arrange on a platter with the toasted baguette slices.

Serves 10–12

33

Macaroni Gratin with Wild Mushrooms

*Wild mushrooms are an extremely popular addition to any bistro repertoire. Here, they
are prepared simply with pasta, shallots and fresh herbs. If good-quality wild mushrooms prove difficult
to find, substitute 9 ounces (280 g) assorted dried ones; reconstitute dried mushrooms in cold water
to cover for a few hours, then drain well and squeeze out any excess liquid before using.*

1½ cups (5 oz/155 g) dried elbow macaroni
2 tablespoons olive oil
2 tablespoons chopped shallots
5 oz (155 g) fresh chanterelle mushrooms, brushed clean and trimmed
4 oz (125 g) fresh shiitake mushrooms, brushed clean and trimmed
2 oz (60 g) fresh oyster mushrooms, brushed clean and trimmed
    Salt and freshly ground pepper
1 tablespoon chopped fresh chives
1 tablespoon chopped fresh parsley
2 cups (8 oz/250 g) finely shredded Swiss cheese

❧ Preheat a broiler (griller).

❧ Fill a large saucepan three-fourths full with water and bring to a boil. Add the macaroni and return to a boil. Cook the macaroni until slightly tender to the bite, about 5 minutes.

❧ Meanwhile, in a large sauté pan over medium low heat, warm the olive oil. Add the shallots and sauté until translucent, about 2 minutes.

❧ Cut any large mushrooms in half. Add all the mushrooms and salt and pepper to taste to the sauté pan and sauté over medium heat until the mushrooms are soft and slightly browned, 4–5 minutes.

❧ When the pasta is done, drain it immediately and add it to the sauté pan holding the mushrooms. Add the chives and parsley and stir to mix. Taste and adjust the seasoning.

❧ Transfer the mixture to a flame-proof 9-inch (23-cm) gratin dish with 2-inch (5-cm) sides or individual gratin dishes. Sprinkle the Swiss cheese evenly over the top.

❧ Place under the broiler just until the cheese melts, about 2 minutes. Serve immediately.

Serves 4–6

Macédoine of Seasonal Vegetables

A macédoine is a mixture of fresh vegetables or fruits, cut into small, uniform cubes.
Use any combination of the vegetables called for here, or include your own favorites.

4   medium-sized artichokes
½   cup (2 oz/60 g) snow peas
     (mangetouts), trimmed
¾   cup (4 oz/125 g) shelled green
     peas
1   cup (5 oz/155 g) shelled fava
     (broad) beans
12   asparagus spears, trimmed
10   baby carrots, peeled
8   small golden beets (beetroots)
½   cup (2 oz/60 g) peeled, cubed
     green apple
2   tablespoons julienned fresh
     basil leaves
3   tablespoons finely chopped fresh
     chives
     Vinaigrette *(recipe on page 13)*
¼   cup (1½ oz/45 g) pine nuts
12   fresh chervil sprigs
     Salt and freshly ground pepper

Using a sharp knife, cut the tops off the artichokes just above the heart. Trim the stems even with the bottoms. Place in a steamer rack over gently boiling water, cover and steam until tender, about 25 minutes. Remove from the steamer and, when cool enough to handle, pull off all the leaves until you reach the pale green hearts. Carefully spread the tender leaves open and, using a small spoon, remove the prickly chokes. Set the cleaned artichoke hearts aside.

Place several ice cubes in a large mixing bowl; fill with water. Set aside.

Fill a saucepan three-fourths full with water and bring to a boil. Add the snow peas and boil until tender, about 3 minutes. Using a small sieve, scoop out the snow peas and immediately plunge them into the ice water to halt the cooking. Remove them from the ice water and set aside.

Toss the peas into the same boiling water and boil until tender, 6–8 minutes. Remove with the sieve, plunge into the bowl of ice water; set aside.

Toss the fava beans into the same boiling water and boil until tender, 3–5 minutes. Scoop them out and plunge them into the ice water. Remove them from the water and, using a small knife, slit the skin on the edge of each bean and "pop" the bean free of its skin. Set aside.

Drain the saucepan, fill it with clean water and again bring to a boil. Add more ice cubes, if needed, to the water in the bowl.

Toss the asparagus into boiling water and boil just until tender, 8–10 minutes. Scoop them out, immediately plunge them into the ice water and then remove them. Set aside.

Toss the baby carrots into the same boiling water and boil just until tender, 5–7 minutes. Plunge them immediately into the ice water, remove them and set aside.

Cut the stems off of the beets above the crown and toss the beets into the same boiling water. Boil just until tender, about 15 minutes. Plunge them immediately into the ice water, then remove them. Using a small knife, peel away the skins.

Cut the artichoke hearts and beets into relatively uniform ¾-inch (2-cm) cubes. Then cut the snow peas, asparagus and carrots into ¾-inch (2-cm) pieces. Combine them all in a large bowl. Add the peas, fava beans, apple, basil and chives. Drizzle on the vinaigrette and mix gently.

Scatter the pine nuts and chervil over the top, season to taste with salt and pepper and serve immediately.

Serves 4

Frisée Salad with Poached Eggs and Pancetta

This savory salad is served plain with only pancetta and croutons or in the style of Lyon, with poached eggs placed on top. The sturdy, curly-edged, bitter frisée lettuce remains an excellent base for either preparation and stands up well when tossed with the warm dressing. If you can't find frisée, spinach is the best substitute.

4   small heads frisée

4   slices pancetta, each about 2 oz (60 g) and ½ inch (12 mm) thick

12 baguette slices, each cut on the diagonal ½ inch (12 mm) thick

4   tablespoons olive oil

4   tablespoons sherry or red wine vinegar

4   eggs

2   tablespoons chopped fresh chives
    Freshly ground pepper

♣ Preheat an oven to 450°F (230°C).

♣ Wash the heads of frisée by soaking them in a bowl of water and then gently lifting them out. Repeat with clean water until the water is clear. Spin or pat the heads dry. Remove and discard the greener outer leaves; keep the whitest parts of the lettuce nearer to the heart, and trim off the tough core. Place the frisée in a large bowl and set aside.

♣ Unroll the pancetta slices and cut crosswise into strips ½ inch (12 mm) thick. Place in a small saucepan with water to cover. Bring to a boil, then remove from the heat. Drain, rinse with cold water; drain again. Set aside.

♣ Brush the baguette slices on both sides with 2 tablespoons of the olive oil and arrange on a baking sheet. Place in the oven and toast, turning once, until the edges are golden brown, 3–4 minutes. Set aside.

♣ Fill a saucepan three-fourths full with water. Add 2 tablespoons of the vinegar and return to a boil. Reduce the heat to medium-low so that the water is just below a boil. One at a time, break each egg into a saucer and slip it into the water. Work quickly so that the eggs all begin cooking at nearly the same time. Poach until the whites appear cooked and are slightly warm to the touch and the yolks are still liquid, about 3 minutes.

♣ Meanwhile, warm the remaining 2 tablespoons olive oil in another sauté pan over medium heat. Add the drained pancetta and sauté until golden brown, about 2 minutes. Add the remaining 2 tablespoons vinegar and deglaze by stirring to dislodge any browned bits from the pan bottom; continue to stir for about 45 seconds. Pour the vinegar mixture evenly over the frisée, add the chives and toss well. Divide the greens evenly among individual plates.

♣ Using a slotted spoon, immediately remove the eggs from the water, shaking off any excess water. Place them on top of the salads.

♣ Add a few turns of ground pepper to each salad and place the toasted baguette slices around the edges of the plates. Serve immediately.

Serves 4

38

Crab Salad with Mango

French chefs have long been innovators when it comes to pairing new and different ingredients. This salad—combining the sweetness of tropical fruit and the spiciness of cayenne pepper with the rich flavor of crab—is the type of dish one might find on the menu of a city bistro, where open markets daily provide a range of fresh and exotic ingredients.

10 oz (315 g) fresh-cooked crab meat, picked over for shell fragments

2 tablespoons mayonnaise

⅔ cup (4 oz/125 g) peeled and finely diced mango

⅓ cup (2 oz/60 g) roasted, peeled and diced red bell pepper (capsicum) *(see glossary, page 124)*

¼ teaspoon cayenne pepper

2 tablespoons chopped fresh chives
Salt and freshly ground black pepper

2 cups (2 oz/60 g) mesclun or other bitter greens

🌿 Wrap the crab meat tightly in a clean kitchen towel to absorb any excess water. Place the crab meat in a bowl and add the mayonnaise. Using a fork, mix together thoroughly.

🌿 Add the mango, bell pepper, cayenne pepper, 1 tablespoon of the chives and salt and black pepper to taste. Mix gently until all the ingredients are evenly distributed.

🌿 Scatter the salad greens evenly over individual plates. Divide the crab mixture equally among the plates, mounding it on top of the greens. Sprinkle the remaining 1 tablespoon chives evenly over the top and serve immediately.

Serves 4

Mussel Salad with Curry Mayonnaise

Curry was not used in French cooking until the early 18th century when the East India Trading Company introduced it to European kitchens. Here, the sharp spiciness of the curry combines with the sweetness of apples as a complement to freshly cooked mussels. Served at room temperature with a very dry white wine, this shellfish salad makes an excellent first course.

1	russet potato, about 10 oz (315 g)
1½	lb (750 g) mussels in the shell, well scrubbed and beards removed *(see glossary, page 126)*
1	cup (8 fl oz/250 ml) water
1	red bell pepper (capsicum), roasted, peeled and seeded *(see glossary, page 124)*
1	large tart, green apple such as Granny Smith, peeled, cored and cut into ½-inch (12-mm) cubes
2	tablespoons minced shallots
1	tablespoon minced fresh basil
3	tablespoons chopped fresh parsley
3	tablespoons mayonnaise
½	teaspoon curry powder
	Salt and freshly ground pepper
4	dashes of cayenne pepper
4	small fresh basil sprigs

⚜ Peel the potato and cut into ½-inch (12-mm) cubes. Fill a small saucepan two-thirds full with water and bring to a boil. Add the potato and boil until tender when pierced with a fork, about 8 minutes. Drain and set aside.

⚜ Discard any mussels that do not close to the touch. In a large saucepan, bring the 1 cup (8 fl oz/250 ml) water to a boil. Add the mussels, cover and steam over high heat, stirring once or twice, until the shells open, 2–3 minutes. Drain the mussels and discard any that have not opened. Remove all but 4 mussels from their shells. Place the shelled mussels in a large bowl; set aside the mussels in their shells to use as garnish.

⚜ Cut the roasted bell pepper into ½-inch (12-mm) squares. Add to the mussels in the bowl, along with the potato, apple, shallots, basil, parsley, mayonnaise, curry powder and salt and pepper to taste. Mix together gently but thoroughly.

⚜ Divide the salad among individual plates and sprinkle each salad with a dash of cayenne. Top each salad with a mussel in the shell and garnish with a basil sprig. Serve immediately.

Serves 4

Fish and Shellfish

ordered on three sides by vast blue waters and punctuated by numerous rivers and lakes, France has traditionally offered a wide range of fresh fish and shellfish on its restaurant menus. Bistros often feature simple shellfish preparations as a first course, with warm, more sophisticated presentations reserved for a small second course to precede the main dish. However, many of the recipes in this chapter will suffice as delectable main course dishes on their own.

The light, versatile flavors of fresh fish and shellfish are deliciously accepting of a variety of different cooking methods, and French chefs find ample ways in which to showcase them. Delicate steamed fillets are natural partners for a mild and creamy sabayon sauce. Sautéed shrimp are combined with the heartier flavors of tomatoes and garlic in the traditional Provençal style. And, because most bistro chefs stress simplicity, you will often find them pairing fresh or steamed *fruits de mer* with simple vinaigrettes or heady blends of fresh herbs.

Basque Calamari Salad

In this spicy salad, calamari is prepared in the Basque style with plenty of tomatoes, red peppers and garlic. To ensure the best flavor, slice the onions and peppers paper-thin, using a mandoline if available, and be sure not to overcook the calamari. Depending on how hungry you are, this salad can be served either as an appetizer or a main course. A chilled dry rosé is a delicious complement.

CALAMARI SALAD
1   lb (500 g) squid
¼   cup (2 fl oz/60 ml) olive oil
2   large red bell peppers (capsicums), seeded, deribbed and very thinly sliced
2   white onions, very thinly sliced
4   cloves garlic, thinly sliced
     Dash of cayenne pepper
     Salt and freshly ground black pepper

SPICY TOMATO VINAIGRETTE
⅓   cup (3 fl oz/80 ml) tomato and red pepper coulis *(recipe on page 14)*
1½   tablespoons sherry vinegar
4   tablespoons chopped fresh parsley
½   teaspoon cayenne pepper
½   teaspoon salt
¼   teaspoon ground white pepper
2   tablespoons olive oil

❧ To make the salad, first clean the squid. Cut off the tentacles above the eyes. Remove the hard round beak lodged in the base of the tentacles by pushing it out. Pull the entrails free of the body and discard. Then pull out the transparent cartilage, or quill, and discard. Rinse the body under cold running water, flushing the body tube well. Using your fingers, pull off the mottled skin covering the body. Cut the body into rings ¼ inch (6 mm) wide. Set the rings and tentacles aside.

❧ In a large sauté pan over high heat, warm the olive oil. Add the bell peppers, onions and garlic and sauté for 2 minutes. Stir in the cayenne and salt and black pepper to taste. Reduce the heat to medium–low, cover and cook, stirring occasionally, until the onions and peppers are very soft, about 30 minutes. Set aside.

❧ Bring a saucepan three-fourths full of water to a boil. Add the squid and cook until just firm, 2–3 minutes; do not overcook. Drain and rinse immediately under cold running water. Drain well and set aside.

❧ To make the vinaigrette, in a large bowl, whisk together the tomato and red pepper coulis, vinegar, parsley, cayenne pepper, salt and white pepper. Add the olive oil and whisk for about 30 seconds until well blended and emulsified.

❧ Add the squid and the onion-pepper mixture to the vinaigrette and toss gently but thoroughly. Taste and adjust the seasoning. Cover and refrigerate for at least 1 hour or for up to 1 day. Serve chilled.

Serves 6 as a first course; 4 as a main course

Lobster Salad with Lemon Vinaigrette

Since its shell turns a deep red during cooking, the lobster has been referred to in France as
"cardinal of the sea." Even were it not for the bright color of their shells, the succulent, dense quality
of lobster meat has made it a king among shellfish often reserved for special occasions.

LOBSTER SALAD

2   live lobsters, 1½ lb (750 g) each
1   teaspoon salt
1   lb (500 g) zucchini (courgettes)
½   cup (3 oz/90 g) peeled, seeded and diced papaya (pawpaw)
½   cup (3 oz/90 g) roasted, peeled and sliced red bell pepper (capsicum) *(see glossary, page 124)*
1   tablespoon fresh tarragon leaves
2   tablespoons julienned fresh basil
1   tablespoon chopped fresh chives

LEMON VINAIGRETTE

3   tablespoons fresh lemon juice
1   teaspoon salt
¼   teaspoon ground white pepper
5   tablespoons (3 fl oz/80 ml) olive oil

❧ To make the salad, first cook the lobster. Fill a stockpot three-fourths full with water and bring to a boil. Slip the lobsters into the water, cover, and cook until the shells are red, about 8 minutes. Using tongs, remove the lobsters and set aside to cool.

❧ When the lobsters have cooled, lay them on their backs on a cutting board. Using a sharp knife and starting at the head end, cut each lobster in half lengthwise. Discard the intestinal vein along the back of the tail. Break off the claws, crack them with a mallet and carefully pull away the shell pieces, leaving the claw meat whole. Remove the tail meat from the shells and set the tail and claw meat aside. Discard the shells.

❧ Place several ice cubes in a large mixing bowl; fill with water. Set aside.

❧ Fill a large saucepan three-fourths full with salted water; bring to a boil.

❧ Meanwhile, trim the zucchini. Then, using a mandoline with the forked shredding attachment or a sharp knife, cut down the length of the zucchini into long, spaghetti-sized julienne strips.

❧ Add the zucchini to the boiling water. When the water returns to a boil, drain the zucchini and plunge it immediately into the ice water to halt the cooking. Drain it again and place in a large salad bowl. Add the papaya, bell pepper, tarragon, basil and chives and toss gently to mix. Set aside.

❧ To make the vinaigrette, in a small bowl, combine the lemon juice, salt and white pepper and whisk together thoroughly. Add the olive oil and whisk for about 30 seconds until well blended and emulsified.

❧ Pour the vinaigrette into the salad bowl, and gently toss all the ingredients together to distribute the vinaigrette evenly.

❧ Divide the zucchini mixture evenly among individual plates. Place a lobster tail half, cut side up, on top of each serving and set the claw meat in the center. Drizzle with any vinaigrette remaining in the bottom of the bowl and serve immediately.

Serves 4

Steamed Mussels with Fresh Herbs

*Along France's northern coast, where mussels prosper in the cold Atlantic waters,
the fresh mollusks are often served with little or no embellishment, save for a sprinkling of
herbs. For a delicious light supper, pair this dish with a side of crisp french fries (recipe
on page 82) and a full-bodied Alsatian wine such as a Gewürztraminer.*

½ cup (2½ oz/75 g) finely chopped shallots

⅓ cup (½ oz/15 g) julienned fresh basil

4 tablespoons fresh tarragon leaves

⅓ cup (½ oz/15 g) chopped fresh chives

⅓ cup (½ oz/15 g) chopped fresh parsley

1½ cups (12 fl oz/375 ml) vinaigrette *(recipe on page 13)*

4 lb (2 kg) mussels in the shell, well scrubbed and beards removed *(see glossary, page 126)*

1 cup (8 fl oz/250 ml) water

½ cup (3 oz/90 g) roasted, peeled and sliced red bell peppers (capsicums) *(see glossary, page 124)*

❧ In a small bowl, combine the shallots, basil, tarragon, chives, parsley and vinaigrette. Stir to mix and set aside.

❧ Discard any mussels that do not close to the touch. In a large saucepan, bring the water to a boil. Add the mussels, cover and steam over high heat, stirring once or twice, until the shells open, 3–5 minutes.

❧ Drain the mussels and discard any that have not opened. Place them in a large serving bowl or divide equally among smaller individual bowls. Scatter the peppers evenly over the top(s).

❧ Pour the vinaigrette-herb mixture directly over the mussels and peppers. Serve immediately or let cool and serve at room temperature.

Serves 4–6

Steamed Salmon with Potato and Garlic Sabayon

Salmon has been popular in French cooking since the Middle Ages, when it was commonly prepared potted, braised or salted, or as an ingredient in ragouts, soups and pâtés. French bistros today prefer to concentrate on its naturally distinctive flavor, often choosing to serve it either steamed or poached. This delicate sabayon sauce adds the wonderfully mellowed flavor of fresh garlic to this simple preparation.

1 russet potato, peeled and cut into eight pieces

8 cloves garlic

4 salmon fillets, about 5 oz (155 g) each, skin removed

Salt to taste, plus ½ teaspoon salt

Freshly ground white pepper to taste, plus ¼ teaspoon ground white pepper

2 tablespoons fresh lemon juice

¼ cup (2 fl oz/60 ml) warm water

¼ cup (2 fl oz/60 ml) olive oil

2 tablespoons chopped fresh parsley or 4 sprigs fresh chervil

In a saucepan, place the potato and add water to cover generously. Bring to a boil and boil until tender when pierced with a fork, about 20 minutes. While the potato is boiling, put the garlic cloves in a separate saucepan, add water to cover and boil until very soft when pierced with the tip of a knife, about 15 minutes.

Meanwhile, sprinkle both sides of the salmon fillets with salt and white pepper to taste and set them aside until you finish preparing the sauce.

Drain both the garlic cloves and the potato and place in a food processor fitted with a metal blade or in a blender. Add the lemon juice, the ½ teaspoon salt, the ¼ teaspoon white pepper and the warm water. Process or blend on high speed just until smooth and creamy, about 20 seconds. Add the olive oil and blend for another 15 seconds to combine. Taste and adjust the seasoning. Set aside, covered.

Place the salmon fillets on a steamer rack over (not touching) gently boiling water. Cover and steam until the salmon is firm, pale pink and opaque throughout when flaked with a fork, about 5 minutes.

Place a fillet of salmon in the center of each of 4 warmed plates. Pour the sauce directly over the fillets, dividing it equally.

Sprinkle each dish with an equal amount of the chopped parsley or garnish with a chervil sprig and serve immediately.

Serves 4

Sautéed Shrimp with Fried Garlic and Baked Tomato

Fresh shrimp, sautéed in butter, garlic and herbs, is a classic bistro standby. In this recipe, baked tomatoes give the dish still more substance and bright color. Vine-ripened tomatoes provide the best flavor. If they are difficult to find, you might consider substituting a bed of steamed spinach in their place. Serve a crusty baguette alongside for sopping up all the delicious juices.

4 tomatoes, about 1½ lb (750 g)
   total weight
   Salt and freshly ground pepper
6 tablespoons (3 fl oz/90 ml) olive
   oil
1 lb (500 g) medium-sized shrimp
   (prawns), peeled and deveined
1 tablespoon finely chopped garlic
1 tablespoon sherry vinegar
2 tablespoons chopped fresh parsley
   Dash of cayenne pepper

☙ Preheat an oven to 450°F (230°C).

☙ Cut the tomatoes in half and place them, cut side up, in a shallow baking dish. Season to taste with salt and pepper and drizzle 2 tablespoons of the olive oil over the tops. Bake until cooked through but still firm, about 15 minutes.

☙ About 3 minutes before the tomatoes are done, in a sauté pan over high heat, warm 1 tablespoon of the olive oil. Add the shrimp and salt and pepper to taste and sauté until pink and firm, 2–3 minutes.

☙ Transfer the baked tomatoes to individual serving dishes. Place the sautéed shrimp on top of the tomatoes, dividing them evenly.

☙ In a small saucepan over high heat, combine the garlic and the remaining 3 tablespoons olive oil and sauté until the garlic turns golden brown, about 1 minute.

☙ Add the vinegar and deglaze the pan by stirring to dislodge any browned bits from the pan bottom, about 30 seconds. Immediately pour the contents of the saucepan equally over each serving. Sprinkle with the parsley and cayenne. Serve at once.

Serves 4

Sea Scallops with Shaved Fennel

The faint aniseed flavor of fresh fennel adds a subtle complement to sautéed sea scallops in this simple dish. The key to this recipe is to slice the fennel paper-thin so that it appears "shaved." Use a mandoline or an extremely sharp knife for the desired effect. Serve this dish hot or at room temperature over a bed of hot white rice, if you like.

2   fennel bulbs
2   teaspoons salt
2   tablespoons olive oil
20   sea scallops, about 1 lb (500 g) total weight
1   cup (8 fl oz/250 ml) tomato and red pepper coulis *(recipe on page 14)*
    Pinch of ground white pepper
½   teaspoon cayenne pepper
2   tablespoons chopped fresh parsley

❧ Remove and discard any bruised outer leaves from the fennel bulbs, then cut off any stalks and feathery tops. Using an electric slicer, a mandoline or a very sharp knife, slice the fennel bulbs crosswise as thinly as possible. Place the fennel slices in a sieve or colander and sprinkle with 1 teaspoon of the salt, tossing the fennel to distribute evenly. Let stand for 30 minutes to drain off any water drawn out by the salt. Then rinse under cold running water and dry thoroughly with paper towels.

❧ In a large sauté pan over high heat, warm the olive oil. Add the scallops and cook, turning once, until golden brown, 1–1½ minutes per side.

❧ Add the fennel and the tomato-pepper coulis and stir well. Then stir in the remaining 1 teaspoon salt and the white and cayenne peppers. Bring to a boil and cook, stirring, until the scallops are firm to the touch, 1–2 minutes longer.

❧ Transfer to a warmed platter or individual plates and sprinkle with the chopped parsley. Serve at once.

Serves 4

Monkfish with Lemon and Coriander Seed

Monkfish is among the ugliest fish to look at, a fact that has earned it the nicknames crapaud (toad) and diable de mer (sea devil) among French cooks and fishermen. Despite its unfortunate appearance, monkfish has a lean, rich and firm flesh that is often compared to lobster meat. Any firm, white fish fillet may be substituted.

2 teaspoons coriander seeds

2 tablespoons fresh lemon juice

2 tablespoons water

¼ cup (1½ oz/45 g) roasted, peeled and chopped red bell pepper (capsicum) *(see glossary, page 124)*

⅓ cup (3 fl oz/80 ml) olive oil

1 teaspoon salt, plus salt to taste

½ teaspoon ground white pepper, plus ground white pepper to taste

4 monkfish fillets, ¼ lb (125 g) each

2 tablespoons chopped fresh parsley

❧ In a blender, combine the coriander seeds, lemon juice, water, bell pepper, olive oil, the 1 teaspoon salt and the ½ teaspoon white pepper. Blend at high speed until smooth and creamy, about 1 minute. Pour the purée through a fine-mesh sieve into a clean bowl. Set aside.

❧ Trim off any thick outer membrane of the monkfish fillets and sprinkle both sides of each fillet with salt and white pepper to taste. Place on a steamer rack over (not touching) gently boiling water. Cover and steam until opaque throughout when pierced with a knife, 6–7 minutes.

❧ Transfer the fillets to warmed individual plates. Spoon the sauce evenly over the top and sides of the fish. Sprinkle with the parsley and serve at once.

Serves 6–8 as a first course; 4 as a main course

58

Steamed Halibut with Braised Leek Vinaigrette

Bistro chefs often pair the sweet flavor of cooked onions with steamed fish fillets. In this recipe, two onion preparations—braised and fried—set this dish apart. Since the fried onions should remain crisp to contrast with the delicate texture of the fish, add them only at the last moment, or serve them on the side for diners to add as they like.

Vegetable oil for deep-frying
1   large white onion
    Ice cubes
1   teaspoon salt, plus salt to taste
2   leeks, halved lengthwise and carefully washed
½   cup (4 fl oz/125 ml) vinaigrette *(recipe on page 13)*
1   tablespoon chopped fresh chives
1   tablespoon chopped fresh parsley
    Freshly ground pepper
4   halibut fillets, about 5 oz (155 g) each

❧ In a deep-fat fryer or a large, heavy-bottomed saucepan, pour in vegetable oil to a depth of 3 inches (7.5 cm). Heat to 350°F (180°C) on a deep-fat frying thermometer, or until a crust of bread becomes golden within moments of being dropped into the oil.

❧ While the oil heats, using a mandoline or a sharp knife, slice the onion crosswise as thinly as possible; you should have about 2 cups (7 oz/220 g). Separate the slices into rings.

❧ Slip the onion slices into the hot oil and stir gently to separate the rings. Fry until golden brown, 10–12 minutes. Using a slotted spoon, remove the onion from the oil and spread them out on paper towels to drain; set aside.

❧ Fill a bowl with ice cubes and water and set aside. Fill a large saucepan two-thirds full with water. Add the 1 teaspoon salt and bring to a boil.

❧ Cut the leeks into ½-inch (12-mm) dice; you should have about 3 cups (12 oz/375 g).

❧ Add the leeks to the boiling water, return to a boil and boil until they are very tender, 4–5 minutes. Drain

and immediately plunge them into the ice water to halt the cooking. Drain again.

❧ In a sauté pan over high heat, combine the cooked leeks and vinaigrette and heat, stirring often, until warmed through, 1–2 minutes. Stir in the chives and parsley. Taste and adjust the seasoning with salt and pepper. Set aside.

❧ Sprinkle both sides of the halibut fillets with salt and pepper to taste. Place on a steamer rack over (not touching) gently boiling water. Cover and steam until opaque throughout when pierced with a knife, about 5 minutes.

❧ Using a slotted spoon, remove the leeks from the sauté pan. Place on warmed individual plates, dividing the leeks evenly.

❧ Place a halibut fillet on top of each bed of leeks. Scatter the fried onion over the fish and serve immediately.

Serves 4

Crispy Fillet of Striped Bass with Pipérade

This true pipérade—a mixture of tomatoes, bell pepper, onions and seasonings—is a signature sauce of the Basque country in southwestern France. The crunchiness of the sautéed skin makes the bass fillets especially flavorful; if you prefer, however, you may remove the skin just before serving.

PIPÉRADE

2	white onions
¼	cup (2 fl oz/60 ml) olive oil
2	green bell peppers (capsicums), seeded, deribbed and thinly sliced crosswise
5	cloves garlic, crushed
2	tomatoes, coarsely chopped
1	teaspoon salt
½	teaspoon ground white pepper
½	teaspoon cayenne pepper
	Pinch of sugar

BASS FILLETS

1	tablespoon olive oil
	Salt and ground white pepper
4	striped bass fillets with skin intact, about ¼ lb (125 g) each

❧ To make the pipérade, using a mandoline or a sharp knife, slice the onions crosswise as thinly as possible. Separate the slices into rings; you should have about 3 cups (10½ oz/ 330 g) rings.

❧ In a sauté pan over high heat, warm the ¼ cup (2 fl oz/60 ml) olive oil. Add the onions, bell peppers and garlic and sauté until the vegetables are soft and golden brown, about 10 minutes.

❧ Add the tomatoes, 1 teaspoon salt, ½ teaspoon white pepper, the cayenne pepper and sugar; stir until blended, then cover. Reduce the heat to medium and continue to cook, stirring occasionally, until soupy, about 15 minutes.

❧ Meanwhile, cook the fillets. In a nonstick sauté pan over high heat, warm the 1 tablespoon olive oil. Sprinkle both sides of the bass fillets with salt and white pepper to taste.

Place the fillets in the hot pan, skin side down, and cook until the skins are crisp and golden brown, 2–3 minutes. Turn the fillets over and continue cooking until opaque throughout when pierced with a knife, 1–2 minutes longer.

❧ Just before the fillets are ready, taste the pipérade and adjust the seasoning if necessary. Spoon the sauce onto the center of a warmed platter or individual plates. Promptly remove the fillets from the sauté pan and lay them, skin side up, on top of the sauce. Serve immediately.

Serves 4

Swordfish Steak with Spinach and Citrus Vinaigrette

Sautéed fish fillet served à la florentine *(on a bed of spinach) is a popular method for preparing seafood throughout France. This particular dish is distinquished by its zesty vinaigrette, which combines three types of citrus with the pan juices. The result is light yet extremely flavorful. A full-bodied white wine such as a white Burgundy would balance the sprightly flavors well.*

¼   cup (2 fl oz/60 ml) water

¼   cup (2 oz/60 g) unsalted butter

5   tablespoons (3 fl oz/80 ml) olive oil

1¼ lb (625 g) spinach leaves, stems removed and carefully washed

Salt and freshly ground pepper

4   swordfish steaks, 5 oz (155 g) each

Juice of ½ orange

Juice of ½ lemon

Juice of ¼ grapefruit

¼   cup (2 fl oz/60 ml) veal stock *(recipe on page 12)* or purchased chicken stock

⚜ In a large saucepan over high heat, combine the water, butter and 2 tablespoons of the olive oil. Once the butter has melted completely, add the spinach leaves and salt and pepper to taste. Cover and cook, stirring every 20–30 seconds, until wilted, about 2 minutes. Remove from the heat and set aside, covered.

⚜ In a large sauté pan over high heat, warm 1 tablespoon of the olive oil. Sprinkle both sides of the swordfish steaks with salt and pepper to taste. Place the swordfish steaks in the hot pan and cook, turning once, until done to your liking, 1–2 minutes on each side for medium-rare. Transfer the fish steaks to a plate and cover to keep warm.

⚜ In a small bowl, stir together the orange, lemon and grapefruit juices.

⚜ Pour off any oil remaining in the sauté pan and place over high heat. When the pan is hot, pour in the citrus juices and deglaze by stirring to dislodge any browned bits from the pan bottom. Boil until the liquid is reduced by half, then add the veal or chicken stock and salt and pepper to taste. Return to a boil and stir in the remaining 2 tablespoons olive oil. Remove from the heat.

⚜ Drain the spinach in a sieve and divide equally among warmed individual plates. Place the swordfish steaks on top of the spinach and spoon the citrus mixture evenly over the steaks. Serve immediately.

Serves 4

Seared Tuna Steaks with Onion Marmalade

Onions, which gained a reputation with the potato as the primary and highly versatile ingredient of the French peasant, reach a new level of refinement in this slow-cooked marmalade for seared tuna steaks. The style in many contemporary bistros is to cook the tuna medium-rare, but you can adjust the doneness to suit your taste. A bed of tender cooked lentils makes a good accompaniment.

ONION MARMALADE

2 slices pancetta, 2 oz (60 g) each, or ¼ lb (125 g) thickly sliced bacon
¼ cup (2 fl oz/60 ml) olive oil
2 large white onions, thinly sliced
½ cup (4 fl oz/125 ml) balsamic vinegar
¼ cup (2 fl oz/60 ml) sherry vinegar
½ cup (4 fl oz/125 ml) water
1 teaspoon salt
¼ teaspoon ground white pepper
2 teaspoons sugar
½ teaspoon cayenne pepper

TUNA STEAKS

4 tuna steaks, about 5 oz (155 g) each
2 tablespoons olive oil
   Salt and ground white pepper

❧ To make the marmalade, first unroll the pancetta, if using. Cut the pancetta or bacon crosswise into strips ½ inch (12 mm) thick.

❧ In a sauté pan over high heat, warm the ¼ cup (2 fl oz/60 ml) olive oil. Add the pancetta or bacon and sauté until slightly crisp, about 2 minutes. Add the sliced onions and continue to sauté until the onions are golden brown, about 10 minutes.

❧ Stir in the balsamic vinegar, sherry vinegar, water, salt, white pepper, the sugar and cayenne. Bring to a boil over medium heat, then continue to boil until the liquid evaporates completely, 12–15 minutes.

❧ About 5 minutes before the marmalade is ready, cook the tuna steaks. In a separate sauté pan over high heat, warm the 2 tablespoons olive oil. Sprinkle both sides of the tuna steaks with salt and white pepper to taste. Place the steaks in the hot pan and cook, turning once, until done to your liking, 1–2 minutes on each side for medium-rare, depending upon the thickness of the steaks.

❧ Transfer the tuna steaks to warmed individual plates. Top with the onion marmalade and serve immediately.

Serves 4

Poultry and Meat

*F*rench chefs are expert in marrying cuts of meat or poultry with the cooking techniques best suited to them. Nowhere is this fact more apparent than in the preparation of the main course. The tougher cuts regularly offered on bistro menus, such as beef short ribs and shoulder of pork or lamb, are made tender by braising or stewing in their juices often with a mixture of vegetables. Leaner meats, such as duck, chicken breast or pork tenderloin, are frequently sautéed or simply broiled as a means of sealing in their own flavorful juices.

Main dish selections traditionally vary according to the region, but most bistro menus are sure to include at least a half-dozen variations on the same French specialties that have been featured in these lively eateries for nearly two centuries. Among the highlights of these classic offerings are the robust cassoulet of Languedoc; whole roasted chicken; perfectly pan-fried steaks accompanied with thin, crisp *pommes frites;* and lightly browned rabbit blanketed in a creamy mustard sauce. Contemporary bistro chefs balance the hearty flavors of old favorites with a host of lighter dishes that make use of the growing availability of fresh ingredients.

Roast Chicken Stuffed with Bread and Garlic

Some type of roast chicken is offered on the menu of nearly every traditional bistro. Here, it is stuffed with thick pieces of bread that have been liberally buttered and rubbed with garlic. The finished stuffing, saturated with the fragrant meat juices, can be served alongside the cooked meat.

1   roasting chicken, about 4 lb (2 kg)
    Salt and freshly ground pepper
6   whole cloves garlic, plus 2 cloves garlic, sliced paper-thin
1   day-old baguette, sliced into strips about 5 inches (13 cm) long and 1 inch (2.5 cm) thick
2   tablespoons unsalted butter, at room temperature
2   sprigs fresh thyme
1   lemon, cut in half
1   tablespoon olive oil
1   cup (8 fl oz/250 ml) water
¼   cup (2 fl oz/60 ml) veal stock or chicken stock *(recipes on page 12)*

♣ Preheat an oven to 450°F (230°C).

♣ Rinse the chicken thoroughly with water and then pat dry with paper towels. Rub inside and out with salt and pepper to taste.

♣ Cut one of the whole garlic cloves in half. Rub the cut sides of the clove over each baguette strip. Spread the strips on all sides with 1½ tablespoons of the butter.

♣ Using the tip of a sharp knife, make at least 12 small incisions in the skin on all sides of the chicken. Slip 1 thin garlic slice into each incision, between the skin and the meat.

♣ Rub the inside of the chicken with the remaining ½ tablespoon butter, and then press the remaining thin garlic slices against the cavity walls. Stuff the bread strips into the chicken cavity and, using kitchen string, truss the chicken by tying the legs together and then tying the legs and wings tight against the body. Tuck the 2 thyme sprigs between the chicken thighs and body.

♣ Place the chicken in a roasting pan, breast side down, and place the lemon halves alongside. Drizzle the olive oil over the chicken and turn breast side up. Scatter the remaining 5 whole garlic cloves around the chicken.

♣ Roast the chicken for 15 minutes. Turn breast side down and roast 10 minutes longer. Add the water to the roasting pan and continue to roast until the juices run clear when the thigh joint is pierced with a knife, 10–20 minutes longer.

♣ Transfer the chicken from the roasting pan to a cutting board. Snip the strings and remove them. Remove the bread from the cavity; arrange it around the edge of a serving platter or place it in a separate dish. Carve the chicken into 8 serving pieces and arrange them in the center of the platter, or place the whole chicken on the platter to carve at the table.

♣ Remove the lemons from the roasting pan. Place the pan over high heat, squeeze the lemons into the pan and deglaze by stirring to dislodge any browned bits from the pan bottom. Add the veal or chicken stock and bring to a boil. Pour the sauce through a fine-mesh sieve into a small serving pitcher.

♣ Place the pitcher of sauce alongside the chicken and serve at once.

Serves 4

Chicken Curry with Green Apple

When curry powder was introduced in France by spice traders in the 18th century, French cooks began to experiment with the highly versatile mix of as many as 10 different ground spices. Curry powders vary slightly from region to region; this recipe calls for a Madras blend, which is one of the best. Serve this quick-to-assemble stew with basmati rice and cold beer.

1   chicken, about 3 lb (1.5 kg)
3   tablespoons olive oil
1   white onion, chopped
1   carrot, peeled and coarsely chopped
1   celery stalk, coarsely chopped
1   cup (8 fl oz/250 ml) dry white wine
1   teaspoon Madras curry powder
2   cups (16 fl oz/500 ml) veal stock or chicken stock *(recipes on page 12)*
    Salt and freshly ground pepper
1   Granny Smith or other tart green apple, peeled, cored and coarsely chopped

🌿 Cut the chicken into 8 serving pieces, discarding the wing tips and the tail.

🌿 In a large sauté pan over high heat, warm 2 tablespoons of the olive oil. Add the chicken pieces and brown on all sides, 2–3 minutes. Add the onion, carrot and celery, reduce the heat to medium-high and sauté until the vegetables are golden brown, about 2 minutes longer. Add the white wine and cook until the liquid evaporates, 5–8 minutes.

🌿 Stir in the curry powder and the veal or chicken stock; bring to a boil. Reduce the heat to medium and simmer, uncovered, until the chicken is cooked through when pierced with a knife, 8–10 minutes longer. Season to taste with salt and pepper.

🌿 Transfer the chicken to a serving dish and cover to keep warm. Continue to simmer the sauce over medium heat until reduced by half, 5–8 minutes longer.

🌿 Meanwhile, in a small sauté pan over medium-high heat, warm the remaining 1 tablespoon olive oil. Add the apple and sauté until tender but firm, 1–2 minutes. Pour the cooked apple over the chicken.

🌿 Strain the reduced sauce through a fine-mesh sieve into a clean container; discard the contents of the sieve.

🌿 Pour the sauce over the chicken and apple and serve immediately.

Serves 4

Breast of Chicken with Carrot and Cumin Broth

French gastronome Brillat-Savarin once said that "poultry is for the cook what canvas is for the painter." Bistro chefs tend to agree, often combining chicken with a wide variety of ingredients and preparations. This dish, pairing chicken breast with the flavors of the Middle East, reflects the light and sophisticated approach of the modern bistro.

6   large carrots, peeled and cut into thin slices
2½ tablespoons olive oil
⅔   cup (2½ oz/75 g) chopped white onion
2   cloves garlic, crushed
1   tablespoon peeled and finely diced fresh ginger
2   tablespoons fresh lemon juice
2   cups (16 fl oz/500 ml) water
½   teaspoon cumin seeds
2   tablespoons chopped fresh parsley
    Salt and freshly ground pepper
4   boneless chicken breast halves, about 6 oz (185 g) each

❧ Fill a saucepan three-fourths full with water and bring to a boil. Add two-thirds of the carrots and return to a boil. Cook the carrots until they are tender when pierced with a knife, about 5 minutes. Drain and set aside.

❧ In a sauté pan over medium-high heat, warm 1½ tablespoons of the olive oil. Add the onion and garlic and sauté until soft and translucent, 3–4 minutes. Add the ginger and sauté for 1 minute longer. Then add the remaining carrots and stir for 30 seconds. Add the lemon juice, water and cumin seeds and bring to a boil. Cover, reduce the heat to medium and simmer until the carrots are tender, 5–7 minutes.

❧ Pour the contents of the sauté pan into a food processor fitted with a metal blade or a blender and process or blend on high speed until smooth, 1–2 minutes.

❧ Pour the sauce through a fine-mesh sieve back into the sauté pan. Add the reserved boiled carrots and the parsley and bring to a boil. Reduce the heat to low, cover and keep warm while you cook the chicken.

❧ In a large sauté pan over high heat, warm the remaining 1 tablespoon olive oil. Rub salt and pepper to taste onto both sides of the chicken breasts. Add the chicken to the hot pan, skin side down, and cook for 1–2 minutes. Reduce the heat to medium and continue to cook the chicken, turning it occasionally, until opaque throughout when pierced with a knife, 12–15 minutes.

❧ Transfer the chicken breasts to the carrot-cumin broth, turning to coat them completely.

❧ To serve, transfer the chicken breasts to warmed shallow bowls and spoon the carrot-cumin broth over the tops.

Serves 4

Duck Leg Confit with Warm Green Lentil Salad

*The tradition of cooking and then storing duck in its own fat goes back to the Moors, who
passed through southwest France in the 8th century A.D. Although confit was once prepared as a means
to preserve meat over long periods of time, it is now prized for its succulence and intense flavor.*

DUCK LEG CONFIT
1	tablespoon salt
1	teaspoon cracked pepper
4	duck legs, about ¾ lb (375 g) each
4	cloves garlic, crushed
4	fresh thyme sprigs
2	bay leaves, torn in half
5	lb (2.5 kg) duck or pork fat, cut into pieces

GREEN LENTIL SALAD
6	cups (48 fl oz/1.5 l) water
1½	cups (10 oz/315 g) dried green lentils
	Bouquet garni (*see glossary, page 124*)
1	teaspoon salt
½	teaspoon freshly ground pepper
1	cup (8 fl oz/250 ml) veal stock or chicken stock (*recipes on page 12*)
	Vinaigrette (*recipe on page 13*)
2	tablespoons chopped fresh parsley

To make the confit, rub the 1 tablespoon salt and the cracked pepper evenly over the duck legs and place in a shallow glass dish. Place 1 clove garlic, a thyme sprig and half of a bay leaf on each leg. Cover with plastic wrap and refrigerate overnight.

The next day, to render the duck or pork fat, place the fat in a heavy-bottomed pan over low heat. Cook slowly until all the fat liquifies, any tissue has become crispy and the impurities sink to the bottom of the pan. This should take 2–3 hours. Pour the clear fat through a fine-mesh sieve lined with cheesecloth (muslin) into a large saucepan.

Cut the duck legs in half to separate the thighs and drumsticks. Place the meat, along with the thyme, garlic and bay leaves, into the melted fat. Bring to a boil, then reduce the heat to medium-low and simmer, uncovered, until the meat is easily pierced with a fork and the juices run clear, about 2½ hours.

Using tongs, carefully transfer the meat to a deep earthenware bowl or terrine. Line a fine-mesh sieve with cheesecloth (muslin) and strain enough of the fat through the sieve to cover the meat completely. Let cool until the fat hardens fully. Make sure that the duck pieces are totally sealed in the fat so that no air can reach them. Cover and refrigerate for at least 24 hours or for up to 3 weeks.

Preheat an oven to 450°F (230°C).

To make the lentil salad, bring the water to a boil in a large saucepan. Rinse the lentils under cold running water. Add the lentils, bouquet garni, the 1 teaspoon salt and the pepper to the boiling water. Reduce the heat to medium, cover and simmer until the lentils are tender, 20–25 minutes.

Meanwhile, remove the duck legs from the fat, scraping off as much of the excess fat as possible. Place the meat, skin side down, in a roasting pan. Place in the oven until the skin is crispy and the meat is hot throughout, about 15 minutes.

When the lentils are cooked, drain them in a fine-mesh sieve. Discard the bouquet garni and place the lentils in a saucepan. Add the stock and vinaigrette and bring to a boil. Stir in the parsley, then taste and adjust the seasoning.

Spoon a bed of lentils onto warmed individual plates and place the hot duck legs on top. Serve immediately.

Serves 4

77

Sautéed Breast of Duck with Wild Mushrooms

The magret *is the large, plumped breast of a mallard or Barbary duck. For especially moist and tender results, allow the cooked meat to rest for at least 5 minutes before slicing so the juices can redistribute through each breast. Use the wild mushrooms called for here, or replace them with your own favorites.*

2   boneless whole duck breasts, about 1 lb (500 g) each
    Salt and freshly ground pepper

¼   cup (2 oz/60 g) unsalted butter

2   tablespoons chopped shallots

2   cloves garlic, crushed and then finely chopped

6   oz (185 g) fresh chanterelle mushrooms, brushed clean, trimmed and coarsely chopped

6   oz (185 g) fresh oyster mushrooms, brushed clean, trimmed and coarsely chopped

5   oz (155 g) fresh shiitake mushrooms, brushed clean, trimmed and coarsely chopped

⅓   cup (3 fl oz/80 ml) dry white wine

1   cup (8 fl oz/250 ml) veal stock *(recipe on page 12)* or purchased beef stock

1   tablespoon chopped fresh parsley

❦ Preheat an oven to 400°F (200°C).

❦ Using a sharp knife, trim off the excess fat from around the edges of the duck breasts. Score the remaining skin covering the breast in a cross-hatch pattern every 1 inch (2.5 cm). Rub salt and pepper to taste onto all sides of the breasts. Place them, skin side down, in an ovenproof sauté pan. Place the pan over high heat and heat until the breasts begin to sizzle loudly, 2–3 minutes. Then slip the sauté pan into the oven and cook for 10 minutes. Turn the breasts over and continue to cook in the oven until firm to the touch, about 5 minutes longer for medium-rare. Remove the duck breasts from the pan and keep warm.

❦ Pour off the fat from the sauté pan. Place the pan over medium-high heat. Add the butter and, when it melts, add the shallots and garlic and sauté just until the shallots are translucent, 1–2 minutes. Add all of the mushrooms and salt and pepper to taste and continue to sauté until the mushrooms begin to soften, 2–3 minutes.

❦ Add the wine and cook until reduced by one-third, about 2 minutes. Add the veal stock and bring to a boil. Reduce the heat to medium and simmer for 5 minutes. Stir in the parsley. Taste and adjust the seasoning.

❦ Meanwhile, cut the duck breasts crosswise on the diagonal into slices ½ inch (12 mm) thick.

❦ Spoon the mushrooms onto a warmed serving platter or individual plates. Arrange the sliced breasts on top. Serve immediately.

Serves 6–8

Rabbit with Mustard and Fava Beans

*Although most common to the Burgundy region, rabbit with mustard sauce is a
bistro favorite throughout France. The addition of fresh fava beans sets this particular
dish apart. Be sure to select beans that are young and tender or use fresh pasta
or peas in their place. This recipe is also delicious prepared with chicken.*

2 tablespoons olive oil
1 rabbit, about 2 lb (1 kg), cut into 8 serving pieces
1 small white onion, diced
4 cloves garlic, crushed
1 cup (8 fl oz/250 ml) dry white wine
1 teaspoon salt
½ teaspoon freshly ground pepper
   Bouquet garni *(see glossary, page 124)*
3 cups (24 fl oz/750 ml) veal or chicken stock *(recipes on page 12)*
   Ice cubes
3 lbs (1.5 kg) fava (broad) beans
2 tablespoons Dijon-style mustard
2 tablespoons julienned fresh basil

🌿 In a large sauté pan over high heat, warm the olive oil. Add the rabbit pieces and brown well, turning once, about 2 minutes on each side. Using tongs, transfer the rabbit to a plate and set aside.

🌿 To the same sauté pan over medium heat, add the onion and the garlic and sauté until they begin to brown, about 2 minutes. Return the rabbit to the pan and add the wine, salt and pepper. Cook over medium heat until the liquid is reduced by half, about 10 minutes.

🌿 Add the bouquet garni and stock to the pan and bring to a boil. Reduce the heat to medium and simmer, uncovered, until the meat falls easily away from the bone, 45–50 minutes.

🌿 While the rabbit is simmering, fill a bowl with ice cubes and water and set aside. Remove the fava beans from their pods and discard the pods. Fill a saucepan three-fourths full with water and bring to a boil. Add the beans to the boiling water and boil for 2 minutes. Drain the beans, then plunge them immediately into the ice water. Remove from the water. Using a sharp knife, slit the skin on the edge of each bean and "pop" the bean free of its skin. Discard the skins and set the beans aside.

🌿 Using tongs, remove the rabbit meat from the sauté pan and place it in the center of a serving platter.

🌿 Strain the sauce remaining in the sauté pan through a fine-mesh sieve directly into a saucepan over medium heat. Add the fava beans and mustard and heat, stirring occasionally, until heated through.

🌿 Pour the sauce over the meat, sprinkle the basil over the top and serve immediately.

Serves 4

81

New York Strip with French Fries

There are few dishes more frequently associated with classic bistro fare than the deliciously simple Steak Frites. To provide the best flavor and texture to pan-fried steak, the meat should be at room temperature at the start of cooking and the pan must be extremely hot when the meat is added.

RED WINE BUTTER
¼ cup (1 oz/30 g) chopped shallots
¾ cup (6 fl oz/180 ml) dry red wine
½ cup (4 oz/125 g) unsalted butter, cut into small pieces
½ teaspoon salt
¼ teaspoon freshly ground pepper

FRENCH FRIES
3 large russet potatoes
  Peanut oil for deep-frying

STEAKS
  Salt and freshly ground pepper
4 New York strip steaks or other tenderloin steaks, about 5 oz (155 g) each
2 tablespoons olive oil

❧ To make the red wine butter, in a small saucepan over high heat, combine the shallots and red wine. Bring to a boil and boil until the liquid evaporates completely, about 10 minutes.

❧ Place the butter pieces in a bowl, and pour the shallots over them. Add the salt and pepper and whisk until no lumps remain. Cover and refrigerate until the mixture is the consistency of butter, about 1 hour.

❧ To make the french fries, peel the potatoes and slice lengthwise ¼ inch (6 mm) thick. Then cut each slice lengthwise into strips ¼ inch (6 mm) wide. Fill a bowl three-fourths full with water and add the potato strips. Let stand for 15–20 minutes, then drain, rinse, and drain again. Repeat the soaking process one more time.

❧ In a deep-fat fryer or a large, heavy-bottomed saucepan, pour in peanut oil to a depth of 3 inches (7.5 cm). Heat to 350°F (180°C) on a deep-fat frying thermometer, or until a crust of bread becomes golden within moments of being dropped into the oil.

❧ Drain the potatoes and pat dry with paper towels. When the oil is hot, working in 2 or 3 batches, slip the potatoes into the oil and fry until they are lightly cooked and soft throughout, 5–7 minutes.

❧ Using a slotted spatula, transfer the potatoes to paper towels to drain. Let cool completely, 15–20 minutes.

❧ Bring the oil back to 350°F (180°C). When it is ready, again working in 2 or 3 batches, slip the potatoes into the oil and fry, turning occasionally, until they are crisp and golden brown, about 6 minutes. Using a slotted spoon, transfer the potatoes to a tray lined with paper towels. Keep warm while you cook the remaining potatoes.

❧ While the final batch of potatoes is frying, prepare the steaks. Rub salt and pepper to taste onto both sides of each steak. In a large sauté pan over high heat, warm the olive oil. When the pan is hot, add the steaks and cook, turning once, until done to your liking, 1½–2 minutes on each side for medium-rare.

❧ Transfer the steaks to warmed individual plates. Spoon 1–2 tablespoons of the butter on top of each steak. Sprinkle the french fries with salt and pepper to taste and place a mound of the hot fries alongside each steak. Serve immediately.

Serves 4

Steak Tartare

*In many of the best French bistros, steak tartare is prepared tableside by a waiter highly
skilled in the art of chopping and mixing the beef, egg and seasonings. The waiter uses no measuring
spoons, making the dish by memory with nothing but a sharp knife and a fork. For superior
taste and texture, use only the knife, rather than a grinder, to chop the fillet.*

1	lb (500 g) beef sirloin, finely chopped *(see note)*
2	tablespoons finely chopped white onion
1½	tablespoons capers, rinsed and well drained
1	egg yolk
1	tablespoon catsup (tomato sauce)
1	tablespoon mayonnaise
2	teaspoons Worcestershire sauce
1½	teaspoons Dijon-style mustard
¼	teaspoon Tabasco sauce or other hot-pepper sauce
1	teaspoon salt
1	teaspoon freshly ground pepper
3	cups (3 oz/90 g) lightly packed mixed salad greens
¼	cup (2 fl oz/60 ml) vinaigrette *(recipe on page 13)*

⚓ Place the chopped beef sirloin in a large bowl. Add the onion, capers, egg yolk, catsup, mayonnaise, Worcestershire sauce, mustard, Tabasco sauce, salt and pepper and, using your hands or a fork, mix together well.

⚓ Divide the meat mixture into 4 equal portions and gently pat each portion between your palms into a patty about 1–1½ inches (2.5–4 cm) thick. Place the patties on the center of individual plates.

⚓ Place the salad greens in a large bowl and drizzle the vinaigrette over the top. Toss to coat evenly. Arrange the mixed greens around the patties on each plate and serve immediately.

Serves 4 as a main course; 6–8 as a first course

Braised Veal Short Ribs with Parsnips

Hearty and comforting braises like this one are always a popular addition to menus during the winter months. The short ribs should be cooked with all the fat intact, as it adds flavor and body to the sauce. If you like, you can remove the fat and bones from the meat just before serving. If parsnips are unavailable, use potatoes instead. Accompany the dish with plenty of fresh bread to soak up any remaining sauce.

SHORT RIBS

3 tablespoons olive oil

3 lb (1.5 kg) veal short ribs

2 carrots, peeled and diced

1 large white onion, diced

1 celery stalk

6 cloves garlic

1 cup (8 fl oz/250 ml) dry white wine

5 cups (40 fl oz/1.25 l) veal stock *(recipe on page 12)* or purchased beef stock

Bouquet garni *(see glossary, page 124)*

1 tablespoon salt

1 teaspoon freshly ground pepper

PARSNIPS

4 parsnips, peeled and cut into thin strips 2 inches (5 cm) long and ¼ inch (6 mm) wide

¾ cup (6 fl oz/180 ml) water

Salt and freshly ground pepper

¼ cup (2 oz/60 g) unsalted butter

2 tablespoons chopped fresh parsley

⚜ To make the short ribs, in a large saucepan over high heat, warm the olive oil. When the pan is hot, add the veal short ribs and brown well on each side, about 2 minutes per side. Using tongs, transfer the short ribs to a plate. Set aside.

⚜ To the same saucepan over medium heat, add the carrots, onion, celery and garlic and sauté until they begin to brown, about 5 minutes.

⚜ Pour the wine into the pan and deglaze by stirring to dislodge any browned bits from the pan bottom. Bring to a boil and return the short ribs to the pan. Add the stock, bouquet garni, salt and pepper and return to a boil. Reduce the heat to medium-low and simmer until the meat begins to fall from the bones, about 1 hour.

⚜ Meanwhile, make the parsnips. In a large sauté pan over high heat, combine the parsnips, water and salt and pepper to taste. Bring to a boil and boil until the liquid evaporates and the parsnips are tender, about 5 minutes. Add the butter and sauté until the parsnips are golden brown, 3–4 minutes.

⚜ Once the meat and vegetables are done, using the tongs, transfer the short ribs to a warmed platter. Strain the juice remaining in the saucepan through a fine-mesh sieve directly over the ribs.

⚜ Arrange the parsnips alongside the meat. Sprinkle the parsley over the ribs and parsnips and serve at once.

Serves 4

Cassoulet

Cassoulet originated in the Languedoc region of southwest France. The main ingredient is always white beans to which are added a variety of different meats according to region. This one, combining lamb with sausage and duck confit, is similar to the classic cassoulets of Toulouse.

Duck leg confit *(recipe on page 77)*
4½ cups (2 lb/1 kg) dried white beans
1 white onion
5 whole cloves
½ cup (4 oz/125 g) rendered duck fat, from preparing the confit
1 carrot, peeled and coarsely chopped
2 celery stalks, coarsely chopped
⅔ cup (3 oz/90 g) garlic cloves (about 2 heads)
1 piece pancetta, ½ lb (250 g), cut into 1-inch (2.5-cm) cubes
10½ cups (84 fl oz/2.6 l) veal stock *(recipe on page 12)*
2 cups (16 fl oz/500 ml) water
½ lb (250 g) smoked ham hock
2 tomatoes, cut into quarters
Bouquet garni *(see glossary, page 124)*
½ teaspoon salt
1 tablespoon whole black peppercorns
2 lb (1 kg) boneless lamb shoulder
2 tablespoons olive oil
1 cup (8 fl oz/250 ml) dry white wine
1 lb (500 g) cooked pork sausage, cut in half lengthwise
½ cup (2 oz/60 g) fine dried bread crumbs

☙ Prepare the duck leg confit; set aside.

☙ Sort through the beans, discarding any misshapen beans or stones. Place in a large bowl, add water to cover generously and let soak overnight. Drain the beans, rinse well; set aside.

☙ Cut the onion in half and chop half of it. Stud the other half with the 5 cloves.

☙ In a large, heavy-bottomed saucepan or stockpot over high heat, warm the rendered fat. Add the carrot, celery, chopped onion, garlic and pancetta and sauté until the vegetables start to brown, about 5 minutes.

☙ Add the white beans, 8 cups (64 fl oz/2 l) of the veal stock, water, clove-studded onion, ham hock, tomatoes, bouquet garni, salt and peppercorns and bring to a boil. Reduce the heat to medium, cover and simmer until the beans are tender but not mushy, about 1 hour.

☙ Meanwhile, trim any excess fat from the lamb shoulder and cut into 1-inch (2.5-cm) cubes. In a large sauté pan over high heat, warm the olive oil. Working in batches, add the lamb and sauté until the meat begins to brown, about 5 minutes. Using a slotted spoon, transfer the meat to a plate and set aside.

☙ Pour off the fat from the pan and return the pan to high heat. When the pan is hot, pour in the wine and deglaze by stirring to dislodge any browned bits from the pan bottom. Return the lamb to the pan, add the remaining 2½ cups (20 fl oz/600 ml) veal stock and bring to a boil. Reduce the heat to medium and simmer until the lamb is tender when pierced with a fork, about 45 minutes.

☙ Remove and discard the clove-studded onion and bouquet garni from the bean mixture. Preheat an oven to 400°F (200°C).

☙ Remove the duck legs from the fat and place on a rack in a baking pan; reserve the rendered fat for other uses. Heat in the oven for 2–3 minutes until the fat melts off.

☙ Add the duck legs, lamb shoulder and sausage to the beans. Bring to a boil and boil for about 3 minutes, stirring gently, to blend the flavors.

☙ Transfer the contents of the pot to a large, heavy-bottomed baking dish, distributing the meats evenly, and sprinkle the bread crumbs evenly over the top. Bake in the oven until browned on top, about 20 minutes. Serve immediately.

Serves 8–10

Drunken Pork Shoulder with Cabbage and Pears

Because pork shoulder is less expensive than the leg or the tenderloin and becomes more tender with long cooking, it is a popular ingredient in the flavorful stews of the French countryside. This "drunken" version features pork marinated and cooked in plenty of robust red wine.

Bouquet garni (*see glossary, page 124*)
2   white onions, diced
2   carrots, peeled and diced
2   celery stalks, diced
3   cloves garlic
30 whole black peppercorns
5   cups (40 fl oz/1.25 l) dry red wine, such as Cabernet or Merlot
    Salt to taste, plus 1 tablespoon salt
3   lb (1.5 kg) boneless pork shoulder, cut into 1-inch (2.5-cm) cubes
6   tablespoons (3 fl oz/90 ml) olive oil
4   cups (32 fl oz/1 l) veal stock or chicken stock (*recipes on page 12*)
1   head green cabbage, thinly sliced
3   tablespoons unsalted butter
¼   vanilla bean (pod), split in half lengthwise
3   ripe but firm pears, such as Comice, cored, peeled and cut into ¾-inch (2-cm) cubes
3   tablespoons chopped fresh parsley

❧ In a large shallow nonaluminum dish, combine the bouquet garni, onions, carrots, celery, garlic, peppercorns, 4½ cups (36 fl oz/1.1 l) of the red wine and salt to taste. Stir to mix. Add the pork and turn to coat evenly. Cover and refrigerate for at least 5 hours or as long as overnight.

❧ Drain the meat and vegetables in a sieve, capturing the marinade in a small saucepan. Bring the marinade to a boil, then remove it from the heat and set aside. Separate the meat from the vegetables; set aside separately.

❧ In a sauté pan over high heat, warm 4 tablespoons (2 fl oz/60 ml) of the olive oil. Pat the meat dry with paper towels. Working in small batches, add the meat to the pan and brown on all sides, about 2 minutes. Transfer the meat to a large saucepan.

❧ To the same sauté pan used for browning the meat, add the reserved vegetables and sauté over medium-high heat until they begin to brown, about 5 minutes.

❧ Transfer the vegetables to the saucepan holding the meat. Add the reserved red wine marinade. Bring to a boil over high heat and boil until reduced by half, about 10 minutes. Add the veal or chicken stock and return to a boil. Reduce the heat to medium and simmer, uncovered, until the pork is tender, 50–60 minutes.

❧ Meanwhile, fill another large saucepan two-thirds full with water, add the 1 tablespoon salt and bring to a boil. Add the cabbage, return to a boil and cook until wilted, about 2 minutes. Drain the cabbage, rinse with cold water and drain again.

❧ In a frying pan over medium heat, melt the butter. Add the cabbage and sauté for 2 minutes. Remove from the heat and set aside.

❧ In another small sauté pan, combine the remaining ½ cup (4 fl oz/125 ml) red wine, the vanilla bean and the pears and bring to a boil. Reduce the heat to medium and simmer, turning the fruit every few minutes, until tender, 5–10 minutes.

❧ Drain the meat and vegetables in a sieve, capturing the juices in a bowl. Cover the juices to keep them warm. Separate the pork from the vegetables; discard the vegetables.

❧ Arrange a bed of the cabbage on a warmed platter. Place the pork on top of the cabbage, and pour the juices over the top. Scatter the poached pear cubes around the meat. Garnish with the parsley and serve at once.

Serves 4–6

91

Roast Pork Tenderloin with Apple-Onion Marmalade

*When pork was introduced in France by the Gauls during the rule of the Roman Empire,
it was considered a meat fit primarily for the common people. These days, advanced farming
techniques produce meat that is far more tender and lean than the original. The best part
of the pork—the tenderloin—is now the basis for a myriad of sophisticated dishes.*

3 tablespoons plus ¼ cup (2 fl oz/ 60 ml) olive oil

1 white onion, thinly sliced

⅓ cup (3 fl oz/80 ml) balsamic vinegar

⅓ cup (3 fl oz/80 ml) sherry vinegar

1 cup (8 fl oz/250 ml) water
Salt and freshly ground pepper

2 pork tenderloins, about ¾ lb (375 g) each

2 fresh thyme sprigs

2 tablespoons unsalted butter

1 small green apple, peeled, cored and cut into ½-inch (12-mm) cubes

3 pitted prunes, thinly sliced

1 cup (8 fl oz/250 ml) veal stock or chicken stock *(recipes on page 12)*

2 tablespoons finely chopped fresh parsley

⚜ In a sauté pan over medium heat, warm the 3 tablespoons olive oil. Add the onion and sauté until golden brown, about 5 minutes. Add the balsamic vinegar, sherry vinegar, water and salt and pepper to taste and cook until the liquid has evaporated and the onions are very soft, about 45 minutes. Set aside.

⚜ Preheat an oven to 450°F (230°C).

⚜ Rub salt and pepper to taste on all sides of the tenderloins. Place them in a roasting pan. Pour the ¼ cup (2 fl oz/ 60 ml) olive oil over the top. Place 1 thyme sprig on each tenderloin.

⚜ Place the pan in the oven and roast the pork for 10 minutes. Turn the pork over and roast until firm and pale pink in the center when cut with a knife, about 10 minutes longer.

⚜ While the pork is cooking, in a large sauté pan over medium heat, melt the butter. Add the apple and prunes and sauté until slightly soft and caramelized, 3–5 minutes. Add the onion marmalade mixture to the pan and continue to sauté until the flavors have blended, 2–3 minutes longer.

⚜ Add the stock to the pan and bring to a boil. Immediately remove from the heat and cover to keep warm.

⚜ When the pork is done, transfer it to a cutting board, cover with aluminum foil and let rest for 5 minutes. Then, using a sharp knife, cut the pork tenderloins into slices ½ inch (12 mm) thick. Arrange the pork slices on a warmed serving platter.

⚜ Spoon the warm marmalade mixture over the pork. Sprinkle with the parsley and serve immediately.

Serves 4

Sautéed Lamb Shoulder with Garlic and Thyme

The combination of lamb with garlic and herbs is a classic European preparation. To vary the recipe, serve it with a variety of different side dishes, such as spicy couscous with garbanzo beans or ratatouille. A red Bordeaux or other hearty, slightly complex wine is always a nice accompaniment.

3 tablespoons olive oil

2 lb (1 kg) boneless lamb shoulder, trimmed of fat and cut into 1-inch (2.5-cm) cubes

½ cup (2 oz/60 g) chopped white onion

1 small carrot, peeled and diced

1 head garlic, separated into cloves and peeled

1 teaspoon salt, plus salt to taste

¼ teaspoon freshly ground pepper, plus ground pepper to taste

1 tomato, coarsely chopped

1 tablespoon finely chopped fresh thyme

1 cup (8 fl oz/250 ml) dry white wine

3 cups (24 fl oz/750 ml) veal stock *(recipe on page 12)* or purchased beef stock

☘ In a large sauté pan over high heat, warm 2 tablespoons of the olive oil. Working in batches, add the lamb and sauté until the meat begins to brown, about 5 minutes. Using a slotted spoon, transfer the meat to a plate and set aside.

☘ Pour off the fat from the pan and place over medium-high heat. Add the remaining 1 tablespoon olive oil to the pan, and, when it is hot, add the onion, carrot and garlic and sauté until the vegetables begin to brown, 4–5 minutes.

☘ Return the lamb to the pan and add the 1 teaspoon salt, the ¼ teaspoon pepper, tomato, thyme and wine. Reduce the heat to medium and cook until the liquid is reduced by half, about 5 minutes. Add the veal stock and bring to a boil over high heat. Reduce the heat to medium and simmer until the lamb is tender when pierced with a fork, about 45 minutes.

☘ Pour the contents of the sauté pan through a fine-mesh sieve into a clean container. Remove the meat and vegetables from the sieve and separate them. Keep the meat warm.

☘ Place the vegetables and all of the strained liquid into a food processor fitted with a metal blade or in a blender and process or blend on high speed until the sauce is smooth, about 30 seconds.

☘ Pour the sauce into a saucepan and rewarm over medium heat. Season to taste with salt and pepper.

☘ Place the lamb on a warmed serving platter or individual plates and pour the warmed sauce over the top. Serve immediately.

Serves 4

94

Desserts

*A*lthough some of the most sophisticated bistros, like the best French restaurants, feature a pastry cart from which diners may select their choice of the daily specialties, most bistro desserts tend toward more homespun fare. In fact, desserts are not a daily selection for most bistro habitués, who instead elect to finish their meals with a bit of cheese and fresh fruit, leaving the sweets for special occasions.

Therefore, when dessert is ordered, it is enjoyed with both great relish and some measure of abandon. In this chapter, you'll encounter several desserts that continue to appear on bistro menus year after year. Fresh fruit, an essential element of the French dessert repertoire, is well represented here by a crisp apple tart and a baked pudding known as clafouti. Even more evident is the generous use of eggs and cream, which show up most delectably in the dense crème brûlée, creamy lemon custard tart and delicate chocolate soufflé.

To cap the meal in truly French style, you might offer a glass of chilled Champagne or a small flute of sweet dessert wine to complement the delicate flavors of your final course.

Crème Brûlée

*Most bistro menus include some variety of this sugar-topped custard. To prevent
the custard from melting while you caramelize the sugar, chill the custard well before you
sprinkle it with the sugar, and broil it just until the sugar melts and browns.*

4   cups (32 fl oz/1 l) heavy (double) cream
1   vanilla bean (pod), split in half lengthwise
7   egg yolks
½   cup (4 oz/125 g) plus 1½ tablespoons sugar for the custard, plus 7 teaspoons sugar for topping

⚜ Preheat an oven to 350°F (180°C).

⚜ In a large saucepan over high heat, combine the cream and vanilla bean and bring to a boil, stirring occasionally with a wire whisk to prevent sticking.

⚜ Meanwhile, in a bowl, using the whisk, stir together the egg yolks and the ½ cup (4 oz/125 g) plus 1½ tablespoons sugar until well blended.

⚜ As soon as the cream boils, immediately pour it in a slow, steady stream into the egg-sugar mixture, whisking constantly.

⚜ Strain the cream-egg mixture through a fine-mesh sieve into 7 ramekins each 3½ inches (9 cm) in diameter and 2¼ inches (5.5 cm) tall, dividing it evenly.

⚜ Place the ramekins in a shallow baking pan and pour in hot water to reach halfway up the sides of the ramekins. Bake until the custard is firm to the touch, about 1 hour and 10 minutes. Remove from the oven and remove the ramekins from the baking pan. Let cool completely, then cover and refrigerate until well chilled, 2–3 hours.

⚜ Preheat a broiler (griller).

⚜ Sprinkle 1 teaspoon of the sugar evenly over the top of each chilled ramekin. Place them on a baking sheet. Place the sheet in the broiler about 4 inches (10 cm) from the heat source and broil (grill) until the sugar caramelizes, about 5 minutes.

⚜ Remove from the broiler and serve immediately.

Serves 7

Mixed Fruit Clafouti

Clafouti, a classic pudding which originated in the Limousin region of France, is traditionally prepared with black cherries. In this recipe, a variety of fruits have been used, but you can incorporate nearly any of your favorites. Sift a dusting of confectioners' (icing) sugar over the top of the cooled cakes before serving, if you like.

½   cup (3 oz/90 g) whole blanched almonds or ⅔ cup (3 oz/90 g) purchased ground almonds

½   cup (4 fl oz/125 ml) milk

½   cup (4 fl oz/125 ml) heavy (double) cream

⅓   cup (3 oz/90 g) plus 1 table-spoon sugar

2   eggs

½   vanilla bean (pod), split in half lengthwise

1   tablespoon unsalted butter

¾   cup (3 oz/90 g) peeled, cored and diced firm green apple

1   mango, peeled, pitted and diced

½   cup (2 oz/60 g) blackberries

⚜ Preheat an oven to 400°F (200°C).

⚜ If you are using whole almonds, place the nuts in a nut grinder or in a food processor fitted with the metal blade. Grind or process until the nuts are a fine powder. (Do not overprocess.)

⚜ In a large bowl, combine the milk, cream, ground almonds, the ⅓ cup (3 oz/90 g) sugar and the eggs. Using the tip of a knife, scrape the seeds from the vanilla bean directly into the bowl. Using a wire whisk, mix until well combined; set aside.

⚜ In a sauté pan over medium heat, melt the butter. Add the apple and the 1 tablespoon sugar and sauté, stirring, until lightly caramelized, 3–4 minutes. Remove from the heat.

⚜ Scatter the apples, mango and blackberries in the bottom of 4 round gratin dishes 5½ inches (14 cm) in diameter. Pour the milk-cream mixture evenly over the fruit.

⚜ Bake until the pudding is set and a knife inserted into the center comes out clean, 20–25 minutes.

⚜ Transfer to a rack and let cool for at least 30 minutes before serving warm.

Serves 4

Sautéed Figs with Roasted Almonds and Cream Mousseline

*Figs are grown throughout the Mediterranean basin and are popular fruits in Italy
and Spain, as well as in France. Sautéing the figs in butter and brown sugar brings out
their full, rich flavor and highlights their wonderfully soft and moist texture.*

SUGAR-ROASTED ALMONDS

4	teaspoons granulated sugar
¼	cup (2 fl oz/60 ml) water
1	cup (4½ oz/140 g) slivered blanched almonds

CREAM MOUSSELINE

½	cup (4 fl oz/125 ml) *crème anglaise (recipe on page 118)*
1	cup (8 fl oz/250 ml) heavy (double) cream

FIGS

2	tablespoons unsalted butter
12	ripe Black Mission figs, cut lengthwise into halves
2½	tablespoons firmly packed brown sugar
	Confectioners' (icing) sugar

To make the sugar-roasted almonds, preheat an oven to 350°F (180°C). In a small saucepan, combine the granulated sugar and water and bring to a boil, stirring to dissolve the sugar. Remove from the heat. Spread the almonds on a baking sheet. Drizzle with the sugar-water syrup and stir well to coat the almonds. Roast, stirring every 5 minutes, until the almonds are pale golden brown, about 5 minutes. (You should have about 1 cup/4½ oz/140 g.) Set aside.

To make the cream mousseline, prepare the *crème anglaise* and set aside. Pour the heavy cream into a large bowl and whisk vigorously until it forms soft peaks. Then add the *crème anglaise* and whisk until combined. Set aside.

To prepare the figs, in a large sauté pan over high heat, melt the butter. As soon as the butter starts to sizzle, add the fig halves and sprinkle with the brown sugar. Sauté, turning the figs gently, until they begin to turn golden brown, 3–5 minutes. Remove from the heat.

Spoon the heavy cream mixture into 4 shallow serving bowls, dividing it equally. Then spoon an equal amount of the figs into the center of each bowl.

Sprinkle evenly with about ⅔ cup (3 oz/90 g) of the sugar-roasted almonds; reserve the remaining almonds for another use. Then sprinkle lightly with confectioners' sugar. Serve immediately.

Serves 4

CHOUX AU CHOCOLAT

Chocolate Cream Puffs

The best cream puffs bake into perfect hollow balls ideal for filling with custard or whipped cream. The dough should be the consistency of thick mayonnaise. If it is too thick, add another egg yolk to achieve the correct consistency. If you like, substitute pastry cream (recipe on page 15) for the chocolate cream, and/or drizzle chocolate sauce over the puffs just before serving.

PASTRY PUFFS
1   cup (8 fl oz/250 ml) water
5   tablespoons (2½ oz/75 g) unsalted butter, cut into small pieces
¼   teaspoon salt
½   teaspoon sugar
1   cup (4 oz/125 g) sifted all-purpose (plain) flour
5   eggs

CHOCOLATE CREAM
13 oz (400 g) semisweet (plain) chocolate, finely chopped
2   cups (16 fl oz/500 ml) heavy (double) cream
¼   cup (2 oz/60 g) sugar

⚜ Preheat an oven to 400°F (200°C). Butter and flour a large baking sheet.

⚜ To make the pastry puffs, in a saucepan, combine the water, butter, salt and the ½ teaspoon sugar and bring to a boil. As soon as it boils, remove the pan from the heat and add the flour all at once. Using a rubber spatula or a wooden spoon, briskly beat in the flour. Place the saucepan over high heat and continue beating briskly for 2 minutes. Remove from the heat again and scrape the contents of the pan into a large bowl. Add 4 of the eggs, one at a time, beating vigorously after each addition until smooth.

⚜ Place the dough in a pastry (piping) bag with a ½-inch (12-mm) plain tip. Pipe mounds about 2 inches (5 cm) in diameter and 3 inches (7.5 cm) apart onto the prepared baking sheet. You should have 16–20 mounds in all.

⚜ In a small bowl, beat the remaining egg until well blended. Using a pastry brush, lightly brush each mound with the egg.

⚜ Bake until the puffs are golden brown, about 30 minutes. Transfer the puffs to a rack and let cool completely, about 30 minutes.

⚜ When the puffs are cool, slice off the top one-third of each puff. Set the bottoms and tops aside.

⚜ To make the chocolate cream, place the chocolate in the top pan of a double boiler or in a heatproof bowl over (not touching) barely simmering water in a pan. Stir just until the chocolate melts, then remove from the heat.

⚜ Pour the cream into a bowl. Using an electric mixer set on high speed, beat until soft peaks form. Add the ¼ cup (2 oz/60 g) sugar and beat until stiff peaks form, about 20 seconds.

⚜ Pour all of the melted chocolate into the whipped cream as quickly as possible, and continue to mix on high speed until evenly combined, about 1 minute.

⚜ Place the chocolate cream in a clean pastry (piping) bag fitted with a ½-inch (12-mm) plain tip. Pipe the cream into the bottoms of the cooled puffs so a little bit of the cream is exposed between the crusts. Replace the tops on the filled bottoms and serve immediately.

Serves 4–6

Chocolate Soufflé

This featherlight soufflé contains no flour, so it is both more chocolatey and more delicate than most others and should be served immediately. Cook it in a large soufflé dish or individual ones; just take care not to fill the dishes more than two-thirds full and adjust the cooking time as necessary.

¼ cup (2 oz/60 g) unsalted butter, melted

2 tablespoons plus ½ cup (4 oz/ 120 g) granulated sugar

3 oz (90 g) unsweetened chocolate, finely chopped

3 egg yolks

5 egg whites
Confectioners' (icing) sugar, optional

⚜ Preheat an oven to 375°F (190°C). Brush the melted butter on the bottom and sides of a soufflé dish 7½ inches (19 cm) in diameter and 4 inches (10 cm) deep.

⚜ Place the prepared soufflé dish in a refrigerator for about 2 minutes, then sprinkle the bottom and sides with the 2 tablespoons granulated sugar, coating evenly.

⚜ Place the chocolate in the top pan of a double boiler or in a heatproof bowl over (not touching) barely simmering water in a pan. Stir just until the chocolate melts, then remove it from the heat. Add ¼ cup (2 oz/60 g) of the remaining granulated sugar, stir to combine, then whisk in the egg yolks. Remove from the heat and let cool.

⚜ Place the egg whites in a clean bowl and, using an electric mixer set on medium-high speed, beat the egg whites until they form stiff but moist peaks. Pour the remaining ¼ cup (2 oz/60 g) granulated sugar into the egg whites and continue to beat until the peaks are stiff and glossy.

⚜ Using a rubber spatula and working in several batches, carefully fold the egg whites into the melted chocolate until no streaks remain. Do not overmix. Pour the mixture into the prepared soufflé dish.

⚜ Bake until the top has risen and is firm to the touch, 20–25 minutes. Sift confectioners' sugar lightly over the top, if desired, then serve at once.

Serves 4–6

Basque Custard Torte

This simple custard-filled cake is native to the Basque region in southwest France. It is often filled with a creamy vanilla custard lightly spiked with the sweet anise flavor of Ricard liqueur, although some areas of the region prefer a filling of black cherries in syrup or cherry jam. To ease unmolding, make sure that the pastry cream is well sealed between the two layers of dough.

½ cup (3 oz/90 g) whole blanched almonds or ⅓ cup (1½ oz/45 g) purchased ground almonds

1 cup (8 oz/250 g) sugar

½ cup (4 oz/125 g) unsalted butter, at room temperature

2 egg yolks

1 tablespoon light or dark rum

1½ teaspoons almond extract (essence)

1½ teaspoons Ricard liqueur
Pinch of salt

½ vanilla bean (pod), split in half lengthwise

1½ cups (7½ oz/235 g) all-purpose (plain) flour

1 teaspoon baking powder

1 cup (8 fl oz/250 ml) pastry cream *(recipe on page 15),* cooled

❧ If using whole almonds, place the nuts in a nut grinder or in a food processor fitted with the metal blade. Grind or process until the nuts are a fine powder. (Do not overprocess.) Set aside.

❧ In a large bowl, using a whisk or an electric mixer set on medium speed, beat the sugar and butter until blended. Beat in the egg yolks one at a time, beating well after each addition. Add the rum, almond extract, liqueur and salt. Using the tip of a sharp knife, scrape the seeds from the vanilla bean directly into the bowl. Mix well.

❧ Add the flour, ground almonds and baking powder. Using a wooden spoon or the paddle attachment of the electric mixer set on low speed, mix well until the ingredients come together to form a firm dough. Shape into a ball, wrap in plastic wrap and refrigerate for 2–3 hours.

❧ Preheat an oven to 350°F (180°C). Butter and flour a cake pan 9 inches (23 cm) in diameter.

❧ On a lightly floured work surface, roll out half of the dough into a round 11 inches (28 cm) in diameter

and ¼ inch (6 mm) thick. Drape the round over the rolling pin and transfer it to the prepared pan. Unwrap the round and press it gently into the pan. Using the rolling pin, roll over the top of the pan to trim away any uneven dough edges. Spread the pastry cream evenly over the bottom of the pastry-lined pan.

❧ Roll out the remaining dough portion into a round about 9 inches (23 cm) in diameter and ¼ inch (6 mm) thick. Place the pan over the dough and, using the pan edge as a guide, cut out a round the size of the pan. Drape the round over the rolling pin and carefully transfer it to the pan, placing it atop the pastry cream, to form the top layer of the cake.

❧ Bake until golden brown, 40–45 minutes. Transfer to a rack and let cool for 10 minutes. Invert onto the rack, turn right side up and let cool completely. Transfer to a serving plate and serve at room temperature.

Serves 8

French Apple Tart

French chefs have been perfecting the apple tart for centuries, creating numerous variations of this classic dessert. This recipe, combining a layer of custard under one of browned apple slices, is one of the most traditional. Brushing the fruit generously with butter before baking will ensure a beautiful golden brown top. Serve warm or at room temperature with crème fraîche or whipped cream, if you like.

Sweet pastry dough *(recipe on page 14)*

5 tart green apples, such as Granny Smith

1 cup (8 fl oz/250 ml) pastry cream *(recipe on page 15),* cooled

2 tablespoons unsalted butter, melted

1 tablespoon sugar

❧ On a lightly floured work surface, roll out the dough into a round 12 inches (30 cm) in diameter and ⅛ inch (3 mm) thick. Drape the dough over a rolling pin and transfer it to a 10-inch (25-cm) tart pan with a removable bottom. Unwrap the dough from the pin and press it gently into the pan. Trim the pastry even with the pan rim and place the pastry-lined pan in the refrigerator.

❧ Preheat an oven to 375°F (190°C).

❧ Peel the apples, then cut them in half and core them. Slice the apples lengthwise as thinly as possible.

❧ Remove the pastry shell from the refrigerator and spread the cooled pastry cream evenly over the bottom of the shell. It should be about ⅛ inch (3 mm) deep. Arrange the apple slices on top of the pastry cream in concentric circles. Brush the apple slices with the melted butter, coating them evenly, then sprinkle with the sugar.

❧ Bake in the oven until golden brown and slightly caramelized, about 50 minutes.

❧ Transfer to a rack and remove the pan sides. Place the tart on a serving plate and serve warm or at room temperature.

Serves 6–8

Goat Cheese Cake

Light and airy with a mild, sweet flavor, this simple cake is a popular choice when the meal does not include a cheese course, because it provides an ideal combination of cheese and dessert. Other fruits, such as quartered fresh figs or nectarines, can be used in place of the berries, if you prefer.

4	eggs, separated
5½	oz (170 g) fresh goat cheese
3	tablespoons sugar
½	cup (4 fl oz/125 ml) crème fraîche
½	cup (2 oz/60 g) fresh raspberries
½	cup (2 oz/60 g) fresh blackberries

🌿 Preheat an oven to 375°F (190°C). Butter a cake pan 8 inches (20 cm) in diameter. Line the bottom with a circle of parchment (baking) paper cut to fit precisely; butter and flour the paper and the pan sides.

🌿 Place the egg whites in a bowl. Using an electric mixer set on high speed, beat the whites until they form stiff but moist peaks.

🌿 In another bowl, combine the goat cheese and sugar and, using a whisk, beat until well blended. Add the egg yolks, one at a time, beating well after each addition until smooth and creamy.

🌿 Using a rubber spatula and working in several batches, carefully fold the beaten whites into the egg yolk mixture. (Do not overmix.) Pour the mixture into the prepared cake pan.

🌿 Bake until the cake is golden, puffed and firm to the touch, about 25 minutes. Transfer to a rack to cool in the pan for 10 minutes, then invert onto the rack, lift off the pan and carefully peel off the paper. Transfer the cake to a serving plate, turn right side up and let cool completely.

🌿 To serve, spread the crème fraîche evenly over the surface of the cake and then top with the berries. Alternatively, cut into wedges and serve warm, topping each piece with a swirl of crème fraîche and some berries just before serving.

Serves 4–6

Lemon Tart

*Bistro dessert carts regularly feature at least one type of citrus tart. This recipe produces
a creamy and tart lemon custard for filling a tender, flaky pastry shell. For a simple variation,
lime or orange juice can be used in place of all or some of the lemon juice.*

1   tablespoon plus ⅓ cup (3 fl oz/
     80 ml) unsalted butter, melted
     Sweet pastry dough *(recipe on
     page 14)*
4   lemons
4   eggs
1¾   cups (14 oz/440 g) sugar
½   cup (4 fl oz/125 ml) water

🌿 Preheat an oven to 400°F (200°C).
Brush the bottom and sides of a
10-inch (25-cm) tart pan with a
removable bottom with the 1 tablespoon melted butter.

🌿 On a lightly floured work surface,
roll out the dough into a round
12 inches (30 cm) in diameter and
⅛ inch (3 mm) thick. Drape the dough
over the rolling pin and transfer it
to the prepared tart pan. Unwrap the
dough from the pin and press it
gently into the pan. Trim the pastry
even with the pan rim.

🌿 Line the pastry-lined pan with
waxed paper and add pie weights or
dried beans. Bake until the pastry is
half-cooked, about 15 minutes.

🌿 Meanwhile, cut 3 paper-thin slices
from the center of 1 of the lemons
and set aside. Into a bowl, grate the
zest from the lemon halves and the
remaining 3 whole lemons. Cut the
whole lemons in half and squeeze
the juice from the halves through a
fine-mesh sieve into a measuring
cup; you should have about ½ cup
(4 fl oz/125 ml) juice.

🌿 Add the lemon juice and eggs to
the zest and whisk until blended. Add
1¼ cups (10 oz/315 g) of the sugar and
mix until well combined. Stir in the
⅓ cup (3 fl oz/80 ml) melted butter.

🌿 As soon as the crust is half-
cooked, remove it from the oven and
immediately remove the pie weights
and waxed paper. Pour the citrus
mixture into the warm tart shell and
return it to the oven. Bake until the
filling is set and the edges are golden
brown, about 20 minutes.

🌿 Meanwhile, in a small saucepan
over medium-high heat, combine the
remaining ½ cup (4 oz/125 g) sugar
and water. Bring to a boil, stirring
constantly to dissolve the sugar. Add
the reserved lemon slices, reduce the
heat to low, and simmer until tender,
about 10 minutes. Remove the pan
from the heat and set aside. When the
tart is done, transfer it to a rack
and remove the pan sides. Let cool
completely.

🌿 Remove the lemon slices from the
sugar-water mixture, shaking briefly
to remove any excess liquid, and
arrange them in an overlapping
pattern on the center of the tart.
Transfer the tart to a serving plate
and serve at room temperature.

Serves 6

Hazelnut and Roasted Almond Mousse Cake

For most French pastry chefs, a good génoise *(sponge cake) is the foundation for dozens of different desserts. This recipe marries the tender cake with a layer of cooked meringue and one of rich hazelnut mousse.*

GÉNOISE
½ cup (4 oz/125 g) sugar
4 eggs
¾ cups (4 oz/125 g) all-purpose (plain) flour

MERINGUE
1 cup (8 oz/250 g) sugar
⅓ cup (3 fl oz/80 ml) water
4 egg whites

HAZELNUT MOUSSE
½ lb (250 g) unsalted butter
¼ lb (125 g) hazelnut (filbert) paste
4 egg yolks
1 cup (8 oz/250 g) sugar
2 cups (9 oz/280 g) sugar-roasted almonds *(double recipe; see page 102)*

❧ Preheat an oven to 400°F (200°C). Butter and flour a cake pan 10 inches (25 cm) in diameter; set aside.

❧ To make the *génoise,* in a large heatproof bowl, combine the sugar and eggs. Place over (not touching) gently simmering water in a pan. Whisk until it feels lukewarm. Remove from the pan and, using an electric mixer set on high speed or a wire whisk, beat until cool and the batter falls in a thick ribbon that holds its shape for 3 or 4 seconds, about 15 minutes. Sift the flour over the batter and, using a rubber spatula, fold it in. Pour into the prepared pan and smooth the top.

❧ Bake just until the cake springs back to the touch, about 20 minutes. Invert onto a rack, carefully lift off the pan and let cool completely.

❧ To make the meringue, in a small saucepan, bring the sugar and water to a boil. Meanwhile, in a bowl, using an electric mixer set on high speed, beat the egg whites until soft peaks form. Continue to boil the sugar-water mixture until it reaches the soft-ball stage, 240°F (115°C) on a candy thermometer.

❧ With the mixer set on medium speed, beat the sugar mixture into the egg whites. Reduce the speed to low, and continue beating until stiff, glossy peaks form, about 5 minutes. Scoop the meringue onto a baking sheet, spread it out in an even layer and refrigerate until cool.

❧ To make the mousse, place the butter in a large heatproof bowl. Place over (not touching) gently simmering water in a pan. Let stand until very soft. Add the hazelnut paste and, using a wire whisk, beat until no lumps remain. Remove from the pan and beat in the egg yolks, one at a time, until creamy. Then gently fold in the meringue.

❧ To assemble the cake, set aside a springform cake pan 10 inches (25 cm) in diameter and 4 inches (10 cm) deep. Using a long, serrated knife, cut the *génoise* to form 3 layers.

❧ Spoon one-third of the mousse over the bottom of the pan. Top with a *génoise* layer. Repeat the mousse and *génoise* layers, ending with a *génoise* layer. Cover and refrigerate until set, about 2 hours.

❧ To unmold, run hot water over a knife blade, wipe dry and slide the blade between the mousse and pan sides. Invert a plate over the pan. Holding the pan and plate together, flip them and lift off the pan. Sprinkle the almonds on the top and sides and serve immediately.

Serves 8–10

Pistachio and Chestnut Cream Mousse Cake

The pleasant green hue of pistachio paste has long made it a popular addition to mousses and ice creams. Look for pistachio paste and chestnut purée in specialty-food shops or prepare your own in a food processor.

Génoise layer, ½ inch (12 mm) thick *(recipe on page 117)*

CRÈME ANGLAISE

1   cup (8 fl oz/250 ml) milk

1   vanilla bean (pod), split in half lengthwise

4   egg yolks, at room temperature

½   cup (2 oz/60 g) granulated sugar

4   gelatin leaves

1   oz (30 g) pistachio paste

2   oz (60 g) chestnut purée

1½   cups (12 fl oz/375 ml) heavy (double) cream

½   cup (2 oz/60 g) finely chopped pistachio nuts

2   tablespoons confectioners' (icing) sugar

🍂 Make the *génoise* as directed and let cool completely.

🍂 To make the *crème anglaise,* in a saucepan, combine the milk and vanilla bean and bring to a boil. Meanwhile, in a large bowl, whisk together the egg yolks and granulated sugar. As soon as the milk boils, remove from the heat. Remove the vanilla bean and, using a knife tip, scrape the seeds into the milk; discard the bean.

🍂 Pour half of the boiling milk into the bowl holding the egg mixture, whisking vigorously. Return the pan to the heat, bring the milk to a boil and pour the egg mixture into the pan, whisking continuously. Stir over medium heat until the custard lightly coats the back of a wooden spoon, 2–3 minutes. You should have about 1 cup (8 fl oz/250 ml). Remove from the heat, press plastic wrap directly onto the surface and let cool.

🍂 Place 2 gelatin leaves in each of 2 small bowls. Add water to cover to both bowls; let stand until softened, about 5 minutes.

🍂 Combine ½ cup (4 fl oz/125 ml) of the cooled custard and the pistachio paste in a blender and mix on high speed until smooth, about 15 seconds. Transfer to a small saucepan over medium heat and heat until warm. Lift out 2 of the gelatin leaves

and add to the warm custard. Whisk to mix well and set aside.

🍂 Put the remaining custard and the chestnut purée in a blender and mix on high speed until smooth, about 15 seconds. Transfer to another small saucepan over medium heat and heat until warm. Lift out the remaining 2 leaves, add to the chestnut custard and whisk well. Set aside.

🍂 In a bowl, place ¾ cup (6 fl oz/ 180 ml) of the cream. Using an electric mixer set on high speed, beat until soft peaks form. Add the pistachio custard and beat on low just until combined, about 30 seconds.

🍂 Place the *génoise* in a springform pan 10 inches (25 cm) in diameter and 2 inches (5 cm) deep. Pour the pistachio custard over the *génoise,* and refrigerate until set, about 10 minutes.

🍂 Whip the remaining cream and beat in the chestnut custard in the same way. Pour the chestnut custard over the set pistachio custard, cover and refrigerate for 4 hours.

🍂 To unmold, run hot water over a knife blade, wipe dry, and slide the blade between the mousse and the pan sides. Release the pan sides and slide the cake onto a plate. Sprinkle on the pistachio nuts and sift the confectioners' sugar over the top.

Serves 8

PARFAIT AU CAFÉ ET À L'ARMAGNAC

Coffee and Armagnac Parfait

This icy dessert combines the pleasure of strong coffee with a shot of good brandy. A base of heavy (double) cream provides a smooth texture, lasting body and stability. For an authentic presentation, serve it in traditional fluted parfait glasses. Cognac or another brandy may be substituted for the Armagnac, if you wish.

⅔ cup (5 oz/155 g) sugar
⅓ cup (3 fl oz/80 ml) water
4 egg yolks
2 cups (16 fl oz/500 ml) heavy (double) cream
2½ tablespoons coffee extract (essence)
⅓ cup (3 fl oz/80 ml) Armagnac
Unsweetened cocoa or roasted coffee beans, optional

🌿 In a saucepan, combine the sugar and water. Stir until the sugar is dissolved; bring to a boil over high heat.

🌿 Meanwhile, place the egg yolks in a heatproof bowl. As soon as the sugar-water syrup boils, remove from the heat and slowly pour the mixture into the egg yolks while whisking vigorously.

🌿 Place the bowl over (not touching) barely simmering water in a pan. Continue to whisk vigorously until the mixture is frothy and stiff, 3–4 minutes.

🌿 Remove the bowl from over the water and, using an electric mixer set on high speed or the whisk, continue to beat until the mixture cools down completely, about 5 minutes. Set aside.

🌿 Place the cream in a large bowl. Using an electric mixer fitted with clean beaters, beat until soft peaks form. Add the coffee extract, Armagnac and cooled yolk mixture and, using a rubber spatula, fold together gently.

🌿 Divide the mixture evenly among 4–6 individual parfait glasses. Cover and freeze for at least 5 hours or, preferably, overnight.

🌿 Serve each parfait garnished with a dusting of cocoa or a few coffee beans, if desired.

Serves 4–6

Chardonnay Sorbet

This refreshing sorbet makes a pleasant finale to a summertime supper. The wine gives it a delicate texture that is at its best just after the sorbet is made. If you like, serve it in chilled glass dishes topped with fresh berries and accompanied with fine French butter cookies. Champagne or sparkling wine can be used in place of the Chardonnay.

1½   cups (12 fl oz/375 ml) water
1½   cups (12 oz/375 g) sugar
½   vanilla bean (pod), split in half lengthwise
½   lime
¼   lemon
¼   orange
4   cups (32 fl oz/1 l) Chardonnay

♣ In a saucepan over high heat, combine the water, sugar, vanilla bean, lime, lemon and orange. Bring to a boil, stirring occasionally to dissolve the sugar. When the mixture begins to boil, reduce the heat to medium and simmer, uncovered, for 5 minutes, to infuse the syrup with flavor. Be sure not to reduce the liquid. Remove from the heat and, using a slotted spoon, scoop out the lime, lemon and orange. Let the citrus fruits cool slightly, then lightly squeeze them over the saucepan to release their juices.

♣ Pour the syrup through a fine-mesh sieve into a bowl. Stir in the Chardonnay, cover and refrigerate for 2–3 hours until well chilled.

♣ Pour the mixture into an ice cream maker and freeze following the manufacturer's directions until the sorbet becomes thick and smooth. The timing will depend upon the type of machine being used.

♣ Remove from the ice cream maker, spoon into chilled serving dishes or glasses and serve immediately, or transfer to an airtight container and store in the freezer for up to 1 day.

Makes about 6 cups (1½ qt/1.5 l); serves 4–6

Glossary

The following glossary defines common ingredients and cooking procedures, as well as special cooking equipment, used in French bistros.

Artichoke
Large flower buds of a variety of thistle. The clusters of tough, pointed, prickly leaves of a mature artichoke conceal tender and gray-green flesh at the vegetable's center—the heart, which cups the prickly and inedible choke.

Baguette
Found in bistros and bakeries throughout France, this traditional white bread loaf is notable for its soft, flavorful crumb, crisp brown crust and long, narrow shape—usually about 2 feet (60 cm) in length and no more than 4 inches (10 cm) or so in diameter.

Bell Peppers
These sweet, bell-shaped red, yellow or green peppers, also known as capsicums, were making their way into French kitchens by the 16th century. Before use, peppers must have their indigestible seeds removed. Often the peppers are roasted, which loosens their skins for peeling and enhances their natural sweetness.

TO SEED A BELL PEPPER
Cut the pepper in half lengthwise and cut or pull out its stem and seeds, along with the white veins, or ribs, to which the seeds are attached.

TO ROAST AND PEEL A BELL PEPPER
Seed the pepper as directed and place the halves, cut sides down, on a baking sheet. Place under a preheated broiler (griller) until the skins blister and turn a deep brown. Remove from the broiler and place the peppers in a plastic or paper bag. Seal and let steam for 10 minutes. Remove from the bag and peel off the skins.

Bouquet Garni
A standard seasoning in simmered savory French dishes, a bouquet garni is any small bundle of fresh or dried herbs tied together to keep them from dispersing in the liquid as they impart their flavor.

TO MAKE A BOUQUET GARNI
For the recipes in this book, place a parsley sprig, a thyme sprig and a bay leaf on a square of cheesecloth (muslin). Bring the corners of the cloth together and tie them securely with kitchen string.

Cayenne Pepper
Commonly used in its ground dried form, this very hot chili lends subtle heat to savory dishes.

Cheeses
"How can you be expected to govern a country that has 246 kinds of cheese?" lamented Charles de Gaulle in 1962. There are, indeed, hundreds of cheeses produced throughout France each year, with local versions on display in regional bistros everywhere.

Goat Generally soft, fresh and creamy, goat's milk cheeses, referred to in France as *chèvre*, are notable for their mild tang. Sold in small rounds or logs (below, left), they are sometimes coated with pepper, ash or herbs, which add subtle flavor.

Roquefort This blue-veined ewe's milk cheese (below, center) comes exclusively from the Aveyron commune of Roquefort-sur-Soulzon. It is prized for its creamy texture and tangy flavor. Substitute any high-quality blue cheese.

Swiss This generic term describes any version of Swiss Emmenthaler (below, right), a firm whole-milk cheese with a yellow color; a mild, nutlike flavor; and distinctive holes that grow larger and more numerous with age.

Chestnut Purée
Often referred to by the French *marrons,* chestnuts are grown in Corsica, the Ardèche, the Dordogne and Lozère. Sweetened chestnut purée, also known as chestnut cream, is a popular ingredient in French desserts. The purée is available in both its sweetened and unsweetened forms in cans or jars in specialty-food shops.

Crème Fraiche
This lightly soured and thickened fresh cream is used by cooks throughout France as a sauce enrichment, topping or garnish for both savory and sweet dishes. It may be found in small tubs in most well-stocked food stores. To make a similar product at home, lightly whip ½ cup (4 fl oz/125 ml) heavy (double) cream; stir in 1 teaspoon sour cream. Then cover and let stand at room temperature until thickened, about 12 hours.

Cumin
With its dusky, aromatic flavor, this Middle Eastern spice may be purchased in the spice section of food stores either as whole, small, crescent-shaped seeds or ground into a powder.

Curry Powder
Dutch and British traders first carried curry powder from India to France in the early 18th century. Most such powders include coriander, cumin, chili powder, fenugreek and turmeric; other additions may include cardamom, cinnamon, cloves, allspice, fennel seeds, ginger and tamarind.

Eggs

For the recipes in this book, use large eggs.

TO SEPARATE AN EGG

Tap the shell on the edge of a bowl and break it in half. Hold the shell halves over the bowl and gently transfer the whole yolk back and forth between them, taking care not to break the yolk; the clear white will drip into the bowl. Transfer the yolk to another bowl.

Extracts

Commercial extracts (essences) are produced by distilling the essential oils of fruits, nuts and other plants, then dissolving them in an alcohol base. Almond, coffee and vanilla are among the most common.

Fava Beans

Variety of fresh or dried bean, also known as broad bean, which resembles an oversized lima bean. Fresh fava beans are sold in their long pods and are easily shelled. Some cooks also remove the tough but edible skin that encases each bean.

Fennel

A crisp, refreshing, mildly anise-flavored bulb vegetable. Its fine, feathery leaves and stems and small, yellowish brown seeds lend fennel's familiar flavor to a wide range of savory recipes.

Foie Gras

The pale, rich, creamy liver—a specialty of Toulouse and Strasbourg—results from force-feeding geese or ducks with corn until their livers swell to a weight of as much as 2 pounds (1 kg) or more. In France, the liver is sold in several forms: raw; freshly cooked; partially cooked and canned; preserved in its own fat; and puréed and canned. For the recipes in this book, use fresh or vacuum-packed foie gras found in some specialty-food stores.

Garlic

Since the time of the Crusades, which spread the use of garlic from the Mediterranean across Europe, this intensely aromatic bulb has been a favorite flavoring in French kitchens.

TO PEEL A GARLIC CLOVE

Place it on a work surface and cover it with the flat side of a large chef's knife. Press down firmly but carefully on the side of the knife to crush the clove slightly; the skin will slip off easily.

Gelatin

Unflavored gelatin gives delicate body to mousses and parfaits. Available in both thin, clear leaves and in a powdered form.

Ginger

This intense sweet-hot spice comes from the rhizome of the tropical ginger plant. Whole fresh rhizomes, commonly but mistakenly called roots, should be peeled before use.

Herbs

Fresh and dried herbs are a popular flavoring agent in French cooking. Some common ones include:

Basil At its best when fresh, this sweet, spicy herb is especially popular in the cooking of southern France.

Bay Leaf The dried whole leaves of the bay laurel tree give their pungent, spicy flavor to sauces, soups, stews, marinades and pickling mixtures.

Chervil With small leaves resembling flat-leaf (Italian) parsley, this herb possesses a subtle flavor reminiscent of both parsley and anise.

Chives Long, thin, fresh green shoots of the chive plant have a mild flavor that recalls the onion, a related plant.

Parsley Fresh parsley is commonly used both to flavor long-simmered dishes and as a garnish. It is available in two varieties: curly-leaf parsley and flat-leaf (Italian) parsley, which has a more pronounced flavor.

Tarragon Fresh or dried, this sweet, fragrant herb seasons salads, seafood, chicken, light meats, eggs and vegetables.

Thyme This delicately fragrant, clean-tasting, small-leaved herb is used fresh or dried to flavor poultry, lamb, seafood and vegetables.

Julienne

French cooking term used to describe both the act of cutting ingredients into long, thin strips and the resulting strips themselves. To julienne an ingredient, cut it lengthwise into thin slices; then, stacking several slices together, slice again into julienne strips. A mandoline or the julienne-cutting disk of a food processor may also be used.

Mandoline

This common French cutting tool—available outside of France in well-stocked kitchen-supply stores—consists of straight and forked cutting blades firmly set at either end of a plastic, metal or wooden frame; some models include a folding stand that holds the frame at roughly a 45-degree angle. To slice vegetables quickly, repeatedly slide them down and up the frame across the blade of choice—a flat edge for slices or a forked edge for julienne.

Mango

Imported into France year-round, this tropical fruit is prized there for its soft, juicy, aromatic orange flesh. A ripe mango will yield slightly to fingertip pressure.

Mushrooms

With their rich, earthy flavors and meaty textures, mushrooms are frequently featured in French cooking. Most varieties are available either fresh or dried. Fresh mushrooms must be cleaned with a soft bristled brush, and dried mushrooms should be rehydrated before using. Some types used in this book include:

Chanterelles In season in France from early summer to early autumn, these subtly flavored, trumpet-shaped, generally pale yellow wild mushrooms (below, right) are usually rapidly sautéed and served in omelets or with light meats. Also known by the French *girolles*.

Oyster Mushrooms These white, gray or pinkish wild or cultivated mushrooms (below, left) have a tender texture and mild flavor faintly reminiscent of oysters.

Shiitakes Especially meaty in flavor and texture, these Asian mushrooms (below, center) have wide, flat, dark brown caps 2–3 inches (5–7.5 cm) in diameter.

Mussels

These popular, bluish black–shelled bivalves have been farmed along the French coast since the 13th century.

TO CLEAN MUSSELS

Before cooking, mussels must be cleaned of any dirt on their shells, and their "beards," the fibrous threads by which they connect to rocks or piers, must be removed. First, holding one under running water, scrub thoroughly with a firm-bristled brush. Then grasp the beard and pull it off. Discard any mussels whose shells do not close to the touch.

Nuts

Bistro cooks make use of a wide variety of nuts in savory and sweet dishes. Some featured in this book include:

Almonds Mellow, sweet-flavored, widely popular oval nuts.

Hazelnuts These spherical nuts, also known as filberts, are used whole, chopped, coarsely ground into a powder or finely ground into a paste. Look for the paste in most specialty-food stores.

Pine Nuts These small, ivory-colored nuts are the seeds of a species of Mediterranean pine tree, and have a rich, delicately resinous flavor.

Pistachios The mildly sweet, full-flavored, crunchy green nuts are native to Asia Minor.

TO TOAST NUTS

Toasting brings out the full flavor and aroma of nuts. To toast any kind of nut, preheat an oven to 325°F (165°C). Spread the nuts in a single layer on a baking sheet and toast until they just begin to change color, 8–10 minutes for most nuts and about 5 minutes for pine nuts. Let cool to room temperature before chopping or grinding.

Oils

French cooks use a variety of oils for sautéing, frying and for making sauces and dressings. Store in airtight containers away from heat and light.

Olive Oil The Romans first brought the olive tree to Mediterranean France, where the oil pressed from its fruit predominates in the cooking to this day. Extra-virgin olive oil, extracted from olives on the first pressing without the use of heat or chemicals, is valued for its distinctive fruity flavor, reflecting the character of the olives from which it was pressed. This character will vary from brand to brand. Products labeled pure olive oil are less aromatic and flavorful and may be used for general cooking purposes.

Peanut Oil This pale gold oil, subtly flavored with the peanut's richness, can be heated to fairly high temperatures and is used by French cooks for deep-frying, as well as for sautéing and in dressings.

Vegetable Oil The term may be applied to any of several refined pure or blended oils pressed or otherwise extracted from any of a number of sources—corn, cottonseed, peanuts, safflower seeds, soybeans, sunflower seeds. Such oils are selected by cooks for their pale color, neutral flavor and high cooking temperature.

Onions, White

These white-skinned, white-fleshed onions tend to be sweet and mild in flavor. If unavailable, substitute with mild yellow onions.

Pancetta

An unsmoked bacon cured simply with salt and pepper, this Italian pantry staple may be found in Italian delicatessens and most well-stocked food stores. It is sold flat or rolled into a large sausage shape (below) from which slices are cut.

Pepper

For the fullest flavor, purchase this common savory spice as whole peppercorns and grind in a kitchen pepper mill or crush coarsely in a mortar as needed. Black peppercorns, which have the most pungent flavor, are picked slightly underripe, and their hulls oxidize as they dry. Milder white peppercorns are fully ripened berries, husked before drying.

Prosciutto

A specialty of Parma, Italy, this raw ham is cured by dry-salting for 1 month, and then it is air-dried in cool curing sheds for 6 months or longer. It has a bright, pink color and deep, salty flavor.

Puff Pastry

This light, flaky pastry—also known as *pâte feuilletée* or *feuilletage*—is made by repeatedly layering pastry dough and butter or another solid fat to form a thin dough that puffs in the oven. Although many types of puff pastry have been made by hand in France for centuries, commercially manufactured frozen varieties are now also available.

Shallots

These small cousins of the onion, grown in France since the 8th century and a special favorite of Bordeaux kitchens, have brown skin, purple-tinged white flesh and a flavor resembling both sweet onion and garlic.

Shrimp

Raw shrimp (prawns) are generally sold with the heads already removed but the shells still intact. Before cooking, shrimp are usually peeled and their thin, veinlike intestinal tracts removed.

TO PEEL AND DEVEIN SHRIMP
Use your thumbs to split open the thin shell along the concave side, between the legs, then carefully peel it away.

Using a small, sharp knife, make a shallow slit along the shrimp's back to expose the veinlike, usually dark intestinal tract (see below). Using the tip of the knife or your fingers, lift up and pull out the vein.

Terrine

A word based on *terre,* "earth," terrine has two meanings in French kitchens. It is a deep, straight-sided ovenproof dish of earthenware, porcelain or glass. The term also refers to mixtures of puréed or chopped poultry, meat, seafood or other ingredients cooked and molded in such containers, then sliced to serve as a first course.

Truffles

Highly aromatic yet subtly flavored, this variety of wild fungus adds distinction to a wide range of savory dishes. The Périgord region of France is the source of what are considered the finest black truffles. Fresh truffles are available in late autumn and winter; they are also sold in jars and cans (whole or in pieces). Peel black truffles before using.

Vanilla Bean

The dried aromatic pod of a variety of orchid, the vanilla bean is a popular flavoring in French and other European desserts. Although vanilla's most common form is that of an alcohol-based extract (essence), the pod and the tiny seeds within it impart an intense vanilla flavor.

TO REMOVE VANILLA SEEDS
Using a small, sharp knife, split the bean in half lengthwise. Then, using the tip of the knife, scrape out the tiny seeds within each bean half.

Vinegar

The term vinegar refers to any alcoholic liquid caused to ferment a second time by certain strains of yeast, turning it highly acidic. Any vinegar will highlight the qualities of the alcoholic liquid from which it has been made. Red wine vinegar, for example, has a more robust flavor than vinegar produced from white wine. Sherry vinegar has the rich, nutlike flavor of the popular fortified wine of Spain. Balsamic vinegar, a centuries-old specialty of Modena, Italy, is made from reduced grape juice and is aged and blended for many years in a succession of casks made of different woods and gradually diminishing in size; the result is a thick, tart-sweet, intensely aromatic vinegar prized by chefs.

ACKNOWLEDGMENTS

Gerald Hirigoyen would like to thank his wife, Cameron, his right hand in developing the recipes for this book. He also extends his heartfelt appreciation to his mother, father, and friend J.B. Lorda, and to the staff of Fringale.

For lending photographic props, the photographer and stylist would like to thank:

Appley Hoare Antiques, Woollahra, NSW

Marchand de Campagne, Paddington, NSW

Ridgway Sassella and Partners, Surry Hills, NSW

Art of Food and Wine, Woollahra, NSW

Howell and Orlando, Woollahra, NSW

Villeroy & Boch, Frenches Forest, NSW

For their valuable editorial support, the publishers would like to thank:
Ken DellaPenta, Liz Marken, Anne Dickerson, Richard Olney, Marguerite Ozburn, Claire Sanchez, Stephani Grant and Laurie Wertz.

PHOTO CREDITS

Pages 2-3:
Grant V. Saint/Image Bank
Pages 6-7:
Eric Berglund/Image Bank
Page 8:
Dave Bartruff
Page 9:
Fred Lyon (top left)
Dave Bartruff (bottom right)
Page 48:
Chris Shorten

Index

BISTRO: THE BEST OF CASUAL FRENCH COOKING